ON MY
HONOR

★ ★ ★ ★ ★ ★ ★ ★ ★ ★ ★

A GUIDE TO SCOUTING
IN THE CHURCH

Meridian
Ward

1

Meridian
Word

1

ON MY HONOR

★ ★ ★ ★ ★ ★ ★ ★ ★ ★ ★ ★

A GUIDE TO SCOUTING IN THE CHURCH

THANE J. PACKER

DESERET
BOOK

SALT LAKE CITY, UTAH

Visit us at deseretbook.com

Library of Congress Catalog Card Number 98-072460

ISBN 1-57008-439-4

Printed in the United States of America   3170-0019R
Alexander's Printing, Salt Lake City, Utah

10   9   8

Contents

Acknowledgments

With sincere appreciation . . .

To Thomas S. Monson and Vaughn J. Featherstone, who over the years have anchored my faith in Scouting as a laboratory for the practice of gospel values by boys of Aaronic Priesthood age.

To Ben E. Lewis who offered a penetrating enrichment of the supporting role which good Scouting offers to the Aaronic Priesthood.

To my daughter, Pamela Packer Smith, who retyped the manuscript in its development and who often retooled some of its features for better presentation.

To my granddaughter, Emily Keith Knell, who so graciously typed and retyped segments of the manuscript as it developed.

To my grandson, Trevor Packer, for his initial encouragement and special attention to its content.

To Andrea Forsythe who gave so graciously a literary housecleaning to the entire manuscript.

To scores of great bishops who knew and understood the program and who forthrightly presented it to their boys as a tool to help validate their callings as the presidents of the Aaronic Priesthood.

To the hundreds of great Scouters and great Primary Scout leaders who, as they lived and worked with and loved boys, became "those of towering strength," to use the words of President McKay.

And lastly to my beloved wife, Palmyra, whose constant love and support, as well as careful management of resource materials, have been a prime factor in this publication.

Introduction

This book had its conception in the shattered expectations of a boy being introduced to Scouting in a small, rural Latter-day Saint ward in northern Utah. A gestation period of many years has followed and been filled with prenatal experiences that produced an impatience for this book's birth. When I was finally encouraged, what might be called a cesarean birth of the book occurred. I hope the reader will be understanding of the simile used in the foregoing description because as a grandfather I find delightful anything that is newborn and in which I can in some way claim inclusion.

The culmination of my boyish dreams came on December 12th at the age of twelve when I became a Boy Scout. My excitement and expectations had been cultivated over several years by my examination and reading of a precious book called the *Scout Handbook*. In the spring of that year I passed my Tenderfoot and Second Class requirements. Successive experiences proved disappointing.

My next Scouting exposure came as a merit-badge counselor for swimming, using facilities of secondary schools in Logan, Utah. I left teaching for a profession with Boy Scouts of America in Berkeley, California, and from there I became the Scout executive of the Cache Valley council, with headquarters in Logan.

While I was in Berkeley, great Scouting was provided for boys by many different institutions. But my experience with Scouting in

the Cache Valley council produced challenging years and deep con-
victions about why Scouting is sorely needed by The Church of
Jesus Christ of Latter-day Saints and why it is so well-equipped to
help Aaronic-Priesthood-age boys develop properly. That Scout
council consisted of seventy-six wards, all sponsors of Scouting.

Those years also helped me recognize how vulnerable Scouting
can be when its method and purposes are not understood by its sponsor. While I was in Cache Valley it also became clear to me that if
Scouting was to play the role for which it was designed by the Boy
Scouts of America, authoritative encouragement by leaders of the
LDS Church was not enough. The purposes and methods of Scouting
had to be clearly understood and vigorously promoted by ward administrators. Parents needed a thorough introduction and a clear understanding of how Scouting was to supplement the activities of the
Aaronic Priesthood quorums. Boys needed vigorous exposure to
Scouting's peer togetherness, its patriotic flavor, and the fun of adventure, particularly outdoor adventure. Above all, *everyone* needed
to understand Scouting's invitation to spiritual development as contained in the Scout Oath, Scout Law, slogan, and motto. It was my
conviction that these ideals could not be presented to boys properly
by following the practices favoring classroom teaching. Rather, they
needed to be presented to boys through an Aaronic Priesthood laboratory closely monitored by skilled and trained quorum advisers acting as lab instructors and occurring at times other than on Sunday.
Scouting is designed to be a laboratory-type experience.

At this time an event occurred that changed the direction of my
life's purpose, a change that would further my understanding of how
Scouting could better serve the needs of Aaronic Priesthood youth. I
was invited by Brigham Young University to become the chairman
of the Department of Scouting Education. The department was introduced into the curriculum of the university to provide opportunities
for young men to find careers with the Boy Scouts of America.
Later, the department expanded and evolved into the Department of
Youth Leadership, covering more areas of interest and including
women in leadership positions. In addition to the department curriculum, three two-hour classes granting general education to all students were included: Cubbing in the LDS Church, Scouting in the
LDS Church, and Exploring in the LDS Church.

To find in a major university a forum for learning that would have a salutary effect upon the youth of America, particularly those of the Aaronic Priesthood, seemed heaven-sent. The opportunity, although not publicly announced by the administration of the university, carried a personal conviction that the most valuable of all contributions Scouting could make to boys was its spiritual strength and the establishment of the importance of the ideals of Scouting in the lives of youth. This was important to boys of all faiths everywhere but especially important to boys who were members of the Aaronic Priesthood of the Church.

Having spent most of my professional career in Scouting, I was fully aware that our young men and their values were challenged from many sources. These challenges had convinced me that the Church desperately needed youth leaders and teachers who could impact the lives of young men when they were not directly under the tutelage of the Church. Once this force was in place, it could add a new dimension of modeling and coaching—a hands-on practice of gospel principles.

My purpose at BYU became to teach, train, and guide young men to choose Scouting as a profession and to help Scouting become a force that would encourage boys to become working exhibits of gospel values on a daily basis. It was my expectation to reach adults, particularly those in positions of priesthood appointment, and enrich their invitation to the youth to try out gospel principles by saying, "Come, follow me. Let us practice the gospel together as we become involved in every wholesome interest in life." Such a leader needs to become literally entwined in the lives of the youth. Such adult mentors would actively participate *with* youth in the doing of gospel principles.

I wholeheartedly sustain the thought that teaching gospel principles by using methods that are largely sedentary, such as Sunday School and seminary, has limitations. A laboratory where Church teachings can be applied is advantageous. Certainly Scouting offers an excellent laboratory-type experience. It is anchored to values that support the ideals of the Church, ideals that become boyhood echoes of the commandments, the Articles of Faith, the scriptures, and pronouncements of the General Authorities—all expressed in language applicable to the growth experiences of youth. Scouting helps boys magnify their stewardships as holders of the Aaronic Priesthood.

Why then the birthing of this book? It is because Scouting is so vulnerable. When Scouting is presented to the sponsoring institution of a ward of the LDS church, Scouting becomes vulnerable because it is designed to help save boys, whereas the ward program is designed to save all of its members. The mix often becomes ill-proportioned at the expense of the Aaronic Priesthood and its laboratory of Scouting. This book will explain why and how this happens and will attempt to suggest how Scouting can better serve the purposes of the Church.

—THANE J. PACKER

1

"Come, Take Up the Cross, and Follow Me"

The introduction of this book pointed out the vulnerability of Scouting when it is sponsored by a church, in this instance The Church of Jesus Christ of Latter-day Saints. However, when Scouting is left free to do its own thing, when the ward sponsor turns Scouting loose and says to its Scout leaders, "Go ahead with your trained leadership and perform as we hope and expect you to perform; do that which you want Scouting to do for your boys," then Scouting becomes far less vulnerable than when it must face the preemptive mind-set of some.

Parenthetically, Scouting will serve its purposes well in the LDS sponsoring situation if the administration of the ward is fully alert to the purposes and methods of the program and if ward leaders can inspire others to provide the necessary kind of leadership. The parents of the boys must also understand Scouting's purposes and methods in order to give boys a clear picture of the appeal of Scouting when it is conducted properly. If these elements are in place, Scouting can provide a special magnification of the Aaronic Priesthood and its purposes.

In the story of our Savior's ministry, the gospel writers refer to the Savior's statement to a follower, "Come, take up the cross, and follow me" (Mark 10:21). I suggest that the reference to the cross which one must take up could include overcoming the vulnerability of Scouting when it is introduced to the wards and their Aaronic Priesthood quorums.

To understand Scouting one must know that it was created in 1908 by Lord Robert S. S. Baden-Powell, the most famous British hero of the time. Scouting challenged boys to be like British heroes such as Lords Nelson, Cook, Clyde, and Livingston. It held high the chivalry of King Arthur and the knights of the Round Table. But why did Scouting spread beyond the borders of Great Britain to boys in every country of the world? It is because the Lord cares for all of his children.

Latter-day Saints see the revelatory wisdom of the Brethren in delivering Scouting to the Aaronic Priesthood quorums of the Church. When properly applied, Scouting acts as a laboratory for boys with dedicated leaders serving as trained laboratory instructors, monitoring and encouraging the application of the purposes of the Aaronic Priesthood by providing action experiences that appeal to quorum members.

First, Scouting succeeds because it supports gospel purposes and yet helps all boys feel accepted in the peer group it creates, attracting both active and inactive boys. It serves as a camouflaged incentive for boys, encouraging them to participate for the sheer joy of it, for the excitement, challenge, action, and adventure.

Second, Scouting succeeds because it contains a code of conduct that appeals to a boy's inborn sense of honor and duty and encourages spiritual development precious to the purposes of the gospel.

Third, Scouting succeeds because it provides an organized magic called the patrol method. This method encourages peer leadership and peer followership, both prime requisites for boy leadership in the quorums and also an important requirement for the successful operation of Scouting itself.

Fourth, Scouting has a patriotic purpose easily equated with the Church's view that we live in a land blessed above all others, a land that provides the right to life, liberty, and religious freedom.

These four characteristics are applicable and meaningful for every LDS boy and can enrich the purposes of the Aaronic Priesthood. Rather than Scouting performing weakly because it is vulnerable. When it performs properly it can successfully support the growth of boys commissioned with the sacred purposes of the Aaronic Priesthood.

The purpose of this book is to examine Scouting as another jewel in the crown of the restored gospel and recognize that when Scouting is given proper direction and purposeful use, it becomes an important laboratory for the Aaronic Priesthood. It provides a splendid tool for Aaronic Priesthood leaders to put their arms around boys and effectively say to them, "Come, follow me."

2

Doctrine & Covenants 107

Section 107 of the Doctrine and Covenants designates the bishop of a ward to be the president of the Aaronic Priesthood. This is a singular directive not found in any other scriptural instruction and as such adds special distinction to his responsibilities.

Fortunate is the bishop who as a boy had a great quorum adviser, someone trained in how Scouting can be used as a laboratory for the quorums. In such instances it is not likely that the assistance Scouting can give to help that bishop achieve the profound spiritual objectives of the Aaronic Priesthood will be neglected. These objectives are so challenging as to suggest that without proper help, a bishop might be required to give the Aaronic Priesthood his entire attention, to the neglect of all other members of his ward.

Through the Aaronic Priesthood, each young man should—

- Become converted to the gospel of Jesus Christ and live by its teachings.
- Magnify priesthood callings.
- Give meaningful service.
- Prepare to receive the Melchizedek Priesthood.
- Commit to, prepare for, and serve an honorable full-time mission when worthy and able.
- Live worthy to receive temple covenants and prepare to become a worthy husband and father.

Such objectives for youth ages twelve to eighteen are so sobering as to frighten even angels. I am reminded of an incident described by Brother Ernest Eberhardt, former mission president and executive secretary to a Presiding Bishopric. While acting as a bishop and Explorer adviser, he led a group of teachers and priests who were in his post on a great adventure up the Beckler River in southern Idaho and on into Yellowstone Park. The second camp was a night to remember because his boys and some bears discovered each other. He remembers thinking, "Lord, if the Aaronic Priesthood has the keys to the ministering of angels, send some now! And send some who aren't afraid of bears!" I suspect that most of us who have become entwined in the lives of boys of Aaronic Priesthood age have had cause to be grateful for any forces the Lord can provide to help us work with them.

These objectives of the Aaronic Priesthood are to be carried out by the bishop, who in addition must be spiritually responsible for all members of his ward. Fortunately, Scouting can provide some important spiritual help if the bishop understands the program and how to use it. With the enormous responsibility a bishop must shoulder, can he say effectively to boys, "Come, follow me"?

First, if you are a bishop, you should know that there are some built-in factors about your calling which may affect your influence on young men. Some would say you start with three strikes against you. Because you represent the Church, you represent all the antiboy demands that are anchored to the LDS Sabbath day. For example, how many of you have a perception that you are a role model for the boys of your ward? Perhaps you may not be, and Sunday, if you will forgive the reference, may be partly responsible. You may be responsible because you represent many constraints that prevent some boys from doing what boys naturally lean toward, simply because they are boys. For the Sabbath, you are saying, "I want you here, sitting in church for three hours. And I do mean sitting!" Strike one? In addition, you are saying, "I want you here sitting and also listening." Listening to what? Too often, it may be listening to speeches and lessons that deal with subjects not chosen out of the natural interests of most boys. Strike two? Not only that, you are asking them to sit and listen for three hours to people giving lessons and speeches that in many instances do not reflect teaching techniques that appeal to boys. Strike three?

Consider how *every* boy in your ward would answer this question: "If you were free to do what you'd like to do on this day, Sunday, what would you do?" How many of your boys would say, "I would like to go to church for three hours"?

Come with me to my office in Logan, Utah, for an experience that touches only the tip of the iceberg of what bishops face in becoming role models. You, the bishop, are there because you have stopped in to talk to me about a ward assignment. While you are there, a young man comes through the door, sees you, and says, "I was told you were here." A delightful exhibit of greeting follows, with physical and emotional manifestations of friendship and positive feelings for one another. The boy has just returned from his mission, and you're seeing each other for the first time. During the course of some conversation that follows, the boy reports that he thought you were a great bishop and that you profoundly influenced him when he was a boy.

In support of that declaration, he says, "Do you know how it started?" Before you can answer, he provides an enlightening justification. "You won't remember this," he says, "but one night at Scout meeting you came while we were playing some games. You showed us how you could jump in the air and kick your heels together three times before landing on the floor. That night I left the meeting thinking you were really something!" Shortly after, the missionary leaves with promises of giving a more detailed report of his mission.

When he has gone, I turn to you and say, "Were you surprised?" You reply, "Oh, yes." And you chuckle as you say, "You know, I thought he was going to tell me about some great spiritual truth that I had spoken of with him, some special gospel principle I had explained, or something related to the traditional expectations of my calling."

Certainly, what transpired between a bishop and a boy on that occasion is not easily identified with the pattern of rubbing off on a boy that takes place on Sunday between a bishop and boys of his Aaronic Priesthood. Within the general image of your calling as a bishop, you should consider that it will be difficult for you to exhibit actions that will make boys of your ward want to be like you. If someone were to ask them who their role models are or who they really liked, would your name be mentioned? Don't become too discouraged—there are many things you can do.

Let's go back to the question of whether a bishop should be someone who says, "Come, follow me." This experience will show more of that iceberg a bishop may not see.

Many years ago a telephone call came to me from a bishop. The conversation went about as follows: "Brother, I have wanted to get in touch with you. We have a group of boys in our deacons quorum who are one-hundred-percenters. They dutifully perform their sacrament assignments every Sunday. They also attend their other meetings. They are fine deacons. We are now concerned that our MIA program is not functioning. We have tried getting a Scout troop going but haven't succeeded. Can we get together and with your help start a better Scout program? The boys are registered, and usually they show up on MIA night and play a little basketball, but that's all."

I was delighted to receive the call but told him there would be a small delay because a summer camp was just beginning. When I mentioned the camp, he was interested. "Would sending the boys to camp be a good start?" he asked. "Perhaps," I responded, "but the ward has to provide its own troop leadership. The camp furnishes only the program specialists." He registered his boys for camp, and with some apprehension I gave him some printed instructions.

Monday came, and I learned that this particular group of boys had checked into camp. Tuesday, an upset mother called me; her motor was really running. I politely listened as she unfolded the following story. Her son, just turned twelve, had called her from a resort close to the camp. The boy was sobbing and expressing emotions of deep trouble. He said that he wanted to come home. When asked why, he said that he wasn't having any fun. In fact, he was having a very bad time. Some of the guys were quarreling. They weren't following camp rules. They were playing poker inside the tents. They were swearing and telling dirty jokes and swiping things from other troops. The food they were trying to cook was terrible. Breaking into the son's story, the mother asked, "For heaven's sakes, where is your Scoutmaster?" The son told her he had brought them over Monday morning and then left to irrigate his farm. "Have you seen your bishop or quorum adviser?" she asked. "No," he reported. They had seen the camp director, but he was very busy.

These were the boys of that one-hundred-percent deacons quorum! These were the boys that lined up every Sunday morning to pass the sacrament. These were the boys who dutifully spent time in quorum meetings listening to the lessons, lessons that were calculated to produce Latter-day Saint behavior in every member of the quorum!

The performance of these boys in this admittedly singular instance prompts questions of how well we reach boys and influence them in formal settings. Could they be expected to be good deacons other than on Sunday? Certainly in this instance they weren't being good Scouts or deacons. Where does being a good deacon begin and end? On Sunday? How many of their Sunday lessons had prompted the need to provide working patterns of LDS behavior other than on Sunday? Can Sunday meetings be enough? Do we dangerously assume that, having performed on Sunday with a sacrament meeting and Sunday School class, the quorum adviser and Sunday School teacher have fulfilled their callings and are then through until next Sunday?

Before we leave the examination of the bishop's task of saying "Come, follow me" to his boys of the Aaronic Priesthood, let me relate an incident that typifies a bishop's challenge as he tries to relate to boys.

On a memorable occasion years ago, it was my privilege to visit an assigned stake while serving as a member of the general board of the MIA. A bishop in that particular stake called me aside during an interval and said, "Brother, several days ago I had an interesting experience that weighs upon me, and I'm curious to know what your reaction would be concerning it." He continued, "The incident occurred on a Sunday when I was leaving the chapel. As I went outside and started toward my car, I ran into a young man who was bouncing a baseball off the side of the church building. He saw me and, recognizing an opportunity, he said, 'Hey, Bishop, will you throw me a couple?' I am a bishop leaving that ward chapel, and here is one of my boys inviting me to spend some time with him and a baseball on Sunday. The boy is a member but very inactive."

As he unfolded the details, I knew exactly what the quandary of any bishop might be in this situation. Straightforwardly I said, "What *did* you do?" He said, "You know, I've worried about that." Purposefully I will not identify what action this bishop took. Certainly he was faced with a challenge.

How can we provide appealing participation for such a boy and boys everywhere in the Church, acceptable experiences, and still hold boys close to the Church? Can we provide a leadership presence that will preserve Sabbath values and still carry boys into manhood without pushing them toward inactivity?

Too often boys can just naturally make things tough for bishops. Consider an incident reported to me by a Scout leader, an incident that occurred during an MIA meeting in a rural ward in Cache Valley. A member of a ward Young Men organization was, as he reported, scolded by his bishop one MIA evening because the boys of Scout age were rowdy and misbehaving. The incident introduced to this Scouter the question, "When is a boy a Scout, and when is he a deacon?" The observation by the bishop included something to the effect that "those darn Scouts are always misbehaving" and that they "are more trouble than they are worth."

It would be appropriate here to relate a story that pointedly describes an attitude felt perhaps by some bishops and other youth leaders, although I can't guarantee the actuality of the event. A contractor was finishing up a day's work by putting the final touches on a cement sidewalk for a home he was building. During the course of the job, the subject of boyhood behavior came up between him and his helper. The contractor thought that boys in general were a lot better behaved than they used to be in his day, particularly on Halloween. He and his helper finished up the sidewalk, troweled it down nicely, and went home.

The next morning when they came back to take the forms off of the project, there was a set of footprints, boy-sized, right down the middle of the sidewalk. Now, this sidewalk was not in front of Grauman's Chinese Theater in Hollywood. The contractor exploded, as one might expect. Here was a relatively expensive project practically ruined. Because the evidence was there, he began to berate this boy, whoever he was. The tirade led to an inclusion of boys of all kinds and all descriptions. The helper, knowing him well enough to comment, said, "Well, now! Wait a minute. I remember you saying just last night that you liked boys. You thought they were pretty good, a lot better than they were when you were their age." The contractor, still obviously upset, retorted, "Yeah, I love them in the abstract, but I hate them in the concrete."

The contractor's response suggests that there is an awkward connection between what boys do and what they ought to do. Those of us who have Sunday assignments often find it difficult to reconcile a boy's natural urges with appropriate Sunday behavior or for that matter with any other appropriate behavior.

Let me share with you an explanation of boys:

About Boys

Show me the boy who never threw
A stone at someone's cat,
Or never hurled a snowball swift
At someone's high silk hat,
Who never ran away from school
To seek the swimming hole,
Or slyly from a neighbor's yard
Green apples never stole.
Show me the boy who never broke
A pane of window glass,
Who never disobeyed the sign
That says, "Keep off the grass."
Who never did a thousand things
That grieve us sore to tell,
And I'll show you a little boy
Who must be far from well.
—Author Anonymous

3

Help for a Bishop

There are some significant things a bishop can and must do to help provide gospel modeling for boys. One is selecting men who will, by virtue of the calling you give them, interact in ways that will profoundly affect boys and save your stewardship. It requires that those men must be able to spend a significant amount of quality time with the boys during their formative years within the arms of the Church as Aaronic Priesthood holders. And this means time spent with boys other than in the sedentary settings prescribed for them during the Sunday meetings. (Would the word *incarceration* be too severe in referring to the formal demands we make upon boys on Sunday?)

Let's spend some time looking at those leaders who must perform as you hope because you have been inspired to call them.

During the priesthood session of the October 1982 general conference, C. Frederick Pingel, bishop of the Beavercreek Ward of the Dayton Ohio East Stake, was invited to speak on the subject of activating young men of Aaronic Priesthood age. He was selected because of the remarkable performance of boys in his ward. His report was so significant and so impressive that I highly recommend it. Bishop Pingel discusses several subjects, among which is the observation that if bishops give top priority to their Aaronic Priesthood boys, they will find a rewarding performance by their youth. Of course, this deals directly with the all-important challenge of selecting brethren as Scout and quorum advisers and people in the Primary who will also represent you. "Fill your youth program with quality people," he pleads. "It's been said that, as you organize a new ward, you first identify your best man and make him your Scoutmaster. Our Scoutmaster is a former bishop. Our Young Men president is a former high councilor. All of our leaders in the Young Men organization served full-time missions; all hold temple recommends. Brethren, don't sacrifice here. . . . Put truly fine people in your youth programs." ("Activating Young Men of the Aaronic Priesthood," *Ensign,* November 1982, p. 35.)

Bishop Pingel didn't mention whether his MIA president also served as Scout leader. Some wards do this when the availability of leaders is limited.

As I listened to this message, I was immediately struck with the unusual ramifications of such a recommendation. Here was a very successful bishop suggesting that before anyone else was called in a ward organization, a bishop should select leaders for his youth, and those leaders were to use Scouting as part of their leadership effort. I thought to myself as I considered the statement, *That surely will not be printed in the conference report.* But when I opened the *Ensign,* there it was as stated.

I think we need to understand what this man was telling us. This bishop was asking for an understanding that youth leaders must be more than teachers of religion classes. The challenge is big!

It is doubtful that there are many boys of Aaronic Priesthood age whose primary interest is in religion. A passive acceptance better describes the majority. Many will become interested in a testimony of the gospel at a later age, but realistically many may not secure a religious experience or seek it until during missionary service.

I think Bishop Pingel understood this. As you read his message, you may agree that he was saying that along with religious teaching the Church must also start at the boys' level of maturity and include that which will challenge their natural interests. Not many of them will show an overriding interest in that which strong members of the Church recognize as important. To me, Bishop Pingel was saying to all bishops and all prospective bishops: Think carefully about who can most effectively reach into the lives of boys and help you as president of the Aaronic Priesthood effectively do all that Doctrine & Covenants 107 asks. Unfortunately, the great scriptures that have to do with generating the truth of the gospel are not easily or naturally applicable to boys. Think of James 1:5–6: "If any of you lack wisdom, let him ask of God, that giveth to all men liberally, and upbraideth not; and it shall be given him. *But let him ask in faith, nothing wavering.* For he that wavereth is like a wave of the sea driven with the wind and tossed." (Emphasis added.)

Or Moroni 10:4: "And when ye shall receive these things, I would exhort you that ye would ask God, the Eternal Father, in the name of Christ, if these things are not true; *and if ye shall ask with a sincere heart, with real intent, having faith in Christ,* he will manifest the truth of it unto you, by the power of the Holy Ghost." (Emphasis added.)

The key to both of these great promises, a key not easily applicable to boys in general, is anchored to the injunctions "But let him ask in faith, nothing wavering" and "Ask with a sincere heart, with real intent, having faith in Christ." Bishop Pingel was warning us that not all boys will want to know at Aaronic Priesthood age and thus will not exercise the desire and faith to learn of religious truths. Not all boys are like the boy Joseph Smith. It is important for bishops to realize this.

Bishop Pingel's reference to Scouting was to suggest that it helps us to start where boys are, where special skills, adventures, excitements, and action interests can also be the focus of effort. I believe he was saying to adult leaders, All of you have a background of very precious experiences that have brought to you the truth of the gospel. However, many boys are not there yet. You can't start where you are; you will succeed better if you start where they are. Then use the special interests they have, capitalize on those as you gain their respect, and blend in or add principles and purposes of the gospel.

Certainly, one reason we have Scouting in the Church is that we need a program which combines boys' interests with priesthood performance and purpose. This explains why we need such special men to lead our youth and why the bishop calls a man to be both quorum adviser and Scout leader.

The word *special* surely describes the type of leader which the bishop must find for his quorums. You will remember Bishop Pingel's injunction at general conference suggesting that before anyone else in the ward is called to serve, the bishop must reserve a man who is to be his Scoutmaster. Where wards are large, three men will be needed to perform as quorum leaders. To find, select, and challenge such men to perform as will be required will demand careful inspiration from the bishop. He will succeed only if he recognizes that such men will be required to devote the kind of time and attention that is required of him. Certainly they, in and of themselves, should possess qualities which the bishop must expect of himself. The selection of the Primary Scout leader will usually not be as difficult. Our Primary Scout leaders have performed remarkably.

Come with me into my home years ago when my youngest son, Rand, was a teacher. His adviser, Glen Tuckett, was the kind of man to which I am referring. He was an assistant coach of the BYU football team and coach of the baseball team. He was one of our best youth leaders. On this occasion, my son Rand was suffering from an attack of the flu. He was coughing, feverish, and feeling low. Yet there he was on Sunday morning, preparing to go to priesthood meeting. With mixed emotions, I counseled him to stay home, indicating his health was important and, perhaps more than anything else, he shouldn't go and expose others. I even went so far as to agree to go to Brother Tuckett and find out about the lesson and bring it home to him. But he was adamant; he wanted to go. I said to myself, *What is this?* This was beyond me. Here he was putting all else aside, even his health, so he could go to priesthood meeting. I was proud of him. This was a demonstration of spiritual strength I had not previously noted in my son. I was amazed. So I kept asking, "Why is it so important to go to priesthood meeting this morning?" He finally said, "Well, Dad, Brother Tuckett is going to tell us all about the football game yesterday!" I was quick to judge. My immediate reaction was to urge him to stay home.

Immediately I looked up Bishop Hintze. The conversation went something like this: "What's going on here? Glen Tuckett will be using the football game for his lesson this morning?" The bishop's response was very humbling for me. He said, "I try to attend those meetings every Sunday. I wouldn't miss them!" I soon found out that every Sunday Brother Tuckett would select a part of an outdoors experience, an athletic contest, or a special event with which he was familiar and which would be of interest to the boys of his priesthood class. He would always find a way to apply it to the point of the quorum lesson that morning. Needless to say, the quorum attendance was one hundred percent in our ward. Every boy of teacher age was active. Brother Tuckett was rubbing off on boys every Sunday morning, teaching them a gospel principle in a remarkable way as well as performing other features required of his calling. He succeeded because he understood boys and had had Scoutmaster training.

Can a bishop find a man of the kind who was singled out by Bishop Pingel? What qualities should he possess? What is it about this man—Scout leader and quorum adviser—who potentially will have a more powerful and profound influence upon a boy than anyone else who may be called by the bishop during his tenure in office, a leader who will especially need to help the bishop hold boys close to the Church until they are ready to accept a call to go on a mission, and whose tenure will hopefully match that of the Bishop?

Perhaps a verse of a poem can introduce this man who performs well for boys.

I'd rather see a sermon than hear one any day;
I'd rather one should walk with me than merely tell the way.
The eye's a better pupil and more willing than the ear,
Fine counsel is confusing, but example's always clear;
And the best of all the preachers are the men who live their creeds,
For to see good put in action is what everybody needs.

I soon can learn to do it if you'll let me see it done;
I can watch your hands in action, but your tongue too fast may run.
And the lecture you deliver may be very wise and true,
But I'd rather get my lessons by observing what you do;
For I might misunderstand you and the high advice you give,
But there's no misunderstanding how you act and how you live.
(Edgar A. Guest, "Sermons We See," in *Masterpieces of Religious Verse,* ed. James Dalton Morrison [New York: Harper & Brothers Publishers, 1948], p. 361)

And another verse about example:

> Example sheds a genial ray
> Of light which men are apt to borrow;
> So, first improve yourself today,
> And then improve your friends tomorrow.
> (Quoted by Heber J. Grant, in Conference Report,
> October 1936, p. 15)

The calling that would fit the appellations of "Come, follow me" and of becoming a good shepherd for a group of boys is profound and so demanding as to deserve the most serious of soul-searching by the recipient. This man will be called to help manage the forces that will truly aid a youngster in beginning the process of being born again during his tenure as holder of the Aaronic Priesthood. This will not necessarily be a magical event that produces a saving experience. Rather it should suggest the recognition that for each boy the process may be slow and extended.

The call to serve as a quorum adviser and Scout leader should not—must not—be equated with the thought of limited service. The bishop might well envision a term of service that he may be projecting for himself. Certainly there should be a recognition that to become trained to lead boys demands a dedicated effort. The management of a group of boys to secure a performance that reflects the skills and ideals so encompassing and profound as those of the Aaronic Priesthood and Scouting requires extensive training and experience, even experimentation. Perhaps more critical is the importance of a one-on-one relationship in which influence, love, and respect are crucial. The success of a spiritual relationship developing between youth and leader begs for an extended period of service. Such challenges suggest a tenure that would match that of the bishop himself, who in calling this man was inspired to make certain that not only was the call made but that the man proved to be chosen. The record of Scouting service in the Church is not always complimentary and bespeaks the vulnerability Scouting faces. The average tenure of the Scout leader in an LDS ward was recently reported as seven months. How tragic for LDS boys as well as for leaders, parents, and bishops.

A Scout leader should be capable of wearing two hats. Wearing one hat he is adviser to the boys in a formal learning style through quorum meetings. As Scout leader he wears the hat of informal learning through Scout activities. This man or woman is the one who will say most literally to boys, "Come, follow me." Who is this person? What is the blueprint for him or her that will produce great blessings for boys when Scouting is combined with the other features of Aaronic Priesthood training and responsibility?

4

Aaronic Priesthood Hero Worship

In a study made within the Youth Leadership department at Brigham Young University, over 2,000 of our young men and women who were sampled reported that the person who did the most besides parents to bring the gospel into their lives and had a profound effect upon them when they were growing up did so in the following ways:

The trait mentioned most often was *personal interest.* The young men's and women's specific observations included: "He really loved me," "She made me feel important," "He always tried to help," "She believed in me," "He really cared."

Understanding was the attribute mentioned next most frequently by these respondents, as in "He understood me or us." Often it was a plurality of reference: "She spoke our language," "He climbed into our world," "She was one with us," "He would listen."

Another attribute very close to understanding was *example:* "His actions matched his words," "She was a model for us," "Every worthy principle was demonstrated at one time or another by him."

Two other traits were often quoted. One was *enthusiasm:* "She never complained," "He really enjoyed being with us," "She had a strong testimony that her calling was important," "He influenced us in spiritual ways."

The other trait was *discipline:* "He was firm, and he made us feel secure," "She always asked us to complete what we started," "He didn't let us take advantage," "She drew the lines on how far we could go," "He insisted that we always do our best, and although he was not condemnatory, he made us understand that he was disappointed if we did not perform the best way we could."

The five aforementioned attributes—*personal interest, understanding, example, enthusiasm,* and *discipline*—are associated with the methods of informal learning. Informal learning is the method that provides, by unstructured experience, the knowing *of* something in addition to learning or knowing or finding out *about* something. By using both aspects of learning, a Primary leader or a quorum adviser and Scout leader can become more effective and truly say to boys, "Come, follow me."

There was an occasion years ago when it was important for another council Scouter and me to make an inspection of a Scout summer camp located in the High Sierra near a lake called Lake of the Woods. The camp was operated by the Presbyterian church of Berkeley, California. Charles M. Wolf was the vice president of safety for the local council, and that spring he invited me to go with him to inspect the camp to make certain that the sanitary facilities had been corrected and were functioning properly. Neither of us had been to the camp, and we stopped in Sacramento to fill up with gas and make inquiries about road designations. As we pulled into a service station, a boy attendant came to us. As he approached the open window, Charles started to speak, but the boy rather politely but enthusiastically interrupted and asked, "Are you a Scoutmaster?" Because Charles was in uniform, the inquiry and the apparent interest of the boy produced further conversation. Charles was more than interested.

The conversation produced a bubbly response by the boy as he excitedly told us about his Scouting activities. I sat quietly listening. When he learned that we were headed for a summer camp, the young man volunteered that his troop was going camping. Charles inquired, "What do you expect to do?" The boy burst forth unforgettably. He said his Scoutmaster knew a place where part of the Donner party had tried to hike across the divide and down to the other side for safety and for help for others of the party. There they had camped for the night, and the fire had eaten down through the very deep snow to a depth over their heads. That night, because of their condition and the deep snow, they died. When winter came the Scoutmaster was going to teach the troop how to survive in the snow.

Charles kept encouraging the boy to talk. He was willing. The Scoutmaster knew of a giant dead tree, one of the biggest in the Sierra. They were going to get permission from the Forest Service to cut it down. They were going to make lunches and place them in position within three feet of where the tree was supposed to fall, and if they didn't succeed in felling the tree within the spot planned, their lunches would all be mashed by the tree. This was quite a Scoutmaster!

They were also going to hike by the stars for a whole night and then camp and come home in the morning after they had panned for gold. The Scoutmaster knew a stream that had a history of gold claims having been filed on it, and they were each going to buy a pan—in fact, the boy had already bought his—and pan for gold. It took us much longer than we had anticipated to secure the gasoline, as we were both so entertained by this young man. When his service was completed, we left with a carefully expressed hope that he would enjoy his Scout camping experience.

A year later I stopped again in Placerville to find the service station where we had met the boy who was so filled with the excitement of Scouting. The station was closed, and no one knew about the boy. I desperately wanted to find out if the dreams that had been cultivated by the Scoutmaster had actually occurred, or if this man was one that "talked a good fight" and then disappointed boys, as is unfortunately often the case in Scouting.

Can you imagine the "Come, follow me" influence of this man if he truly knew what his position as Scoutmaster meant? What if he sought teaching moments when the precious character-building concepts of one's honor and its importance were part of his opportunity? Would he then have had reason to call attention to achievements of trustworthiness, loyalty, and so on? And could he also have instilled the precious concept of a Heavenly Father in their lives, of revering Him and performing reverential duties in a church of their preference?

One example of such a Scoutmaster was shared by Kent McKay at a Great Salt Lake Scouting council almost twenty years ago:

Much of what I've learned in Scouting I've learned in the mountains. I've hiked down to the bottom of the Grand Canyon; I've hiked to the top of the mountains at King's Peak. . . . I've explored new mountains, hiked the wrong mountains, and even got to know the mountains in my own backyard. Now, those journeys into the mountains were hard, but I know that my Scoutmaster did not mean for them to be easy. He wanted us to stretch, and struggle, and learn the lessons of life. Through it all, we learned the importance of having the right attitude.

Our Scoutmaster had been a Scoutmaster for about ten years, and during those years not a single scout in Troop 112 had escaped memorizing scriptures. There's that famous scripture our Scoutmaster calls David O. McKay 2:4: "Tell me what you think about when you don't have to think, and I will tell you what you are and largely what you will become." Our Scoutmaster has a few sayings of his own. Some of them have become legends by now because he says them on every trip, every day, for decades now.

I remember when we were camped at the bottom of the Grand Canyon, and we were supposed to get up early, get organized, and make our way out of the canyon. But we lazied around a little, and soon found ourselves struggling up in the hot sun. Then came that famous saying, "He who can beat the battle of the bed can win the war of the world." In other words, if we are to succeed, we must have self-discipline. That meant getting out of bed in the morning, it meant having control of ourselves. When we didn't do this, when we weren't in control, we had to suffer the consequences. We were too hot, too tired, and too thirsty. Many of the canteens ran out of water before the Scouts got out of the canyon.

Another hike I'll never forget was our hike to King's Peak. We learned the truth of the saying. "When you see a man on top of a mountain, remember, he didn't fall there." After long days of heavy backpacking, just putting one foot in front of the other was hard. That's when I would hear my Scoutmaster say, "Come on now. You'll get your second wind. It's just around the corner. Only 200 yards, more or less. Make your mind tell your body what to do. Don't let your body tell your mind what to do." After we had gone around another corner, and then another and another, after we had gone 200 more yards, 200 more times, just when we thought we were about to drop dead, our Scoutmaster's voice would ring down the mountain, "Boy, this is really livin'!" He'd say it over and over, and then we'd say it, and then it was true. It was really livin'!

There were other things I learned on those trips, scriptures that took on meaning. "Wherefore, be not weary in well-doing, for ye are laying the foundation of a great work. And out of small things procedeth that which is great." One step at a time can finally lead a person to the end of a long journey. And as he goes along the way he should be able to help a friend, because when you help someone to the top of a mountain, you will find that you have also arrived there. On those trips our Scoutmaster talked about more than just merit badges. He talked about the Apostle Paul as we were hiking, and Nephi as we were sitting around the fire, and Abraham as we were gazing up into the stars, and Jesus of Nazareth just before we went to bed. And at one time or another each of us had an opportunity to go out and pray, as Joseph Smith had first prayed.

I listened very closely and tried to do what my Scoutmaster said because I had three older brothers who were Eagle Scouts. I wanted to be like them. My Scoutmaster, well, he was my father, and I wanted to be like him. Now, if I can remember all that I've learned on those trips, up, over, and down, and into the mountains, I believe I can make it through the journey of life. The journey will not be easy, my Scoutmaster knew that. But perhaps, someday, in school, college, on a mission, or sometime later in life if ever I'm discouraged or doubt myself or wonder if I can take another step, I believe those words will come back to me, "Come on now." "You'll get your second wind." "It's just around the corner." "Only 200 yards more." "Make your mind tell your body what to do." "Tell me what you think about when you don't have to think." "Be not weary in well-doing." "Boy?? This is really livin'!" And one more great scripture, "Wherefore, dispute not because ye see not, for ye can receive no witness until after the trial of your faith." The trials will come, but you and I need not be afraid. The Scout Oath and the Scout Law tell us to follow a higher road, to have the right attitude, to serve, to share, and to succeed. We can have the courage to say what President Spencer W. Kimball has said: "There are great challenges ahead of us, giant opportunities to be met. I welcome that exciting prospect, and feel to say to the Lord humbly, 'Give me this mountain.'" (Transcribed by author from tape of council meeting, 13 February 1981.)

Application of Learning

There is a key beyond attendance at meetings on Sunday to insure successful learning. The important one is application. This is best explained and best understood if we clearly recognize the elements that take place in the learning process. We expect boys to come to church on Sunday and to learn about the gospel, but there are limitations to the learning that occurs. The steps include exposure, repetition, understanding, conviction, and last but most important, application. There are a variety of formulas for learning, but most of those proposed by educators include those five steps or variants of them. All such formulas end with application.

The learning processes that take place for boys as they go to church on Sunday use exposure followed by repetition, and understanding is taught as a third step. Verbal sharing and discussion are often used for better understanding. If the teaching is done well, there is even some opportunity to produce conviction. That fourth step uses testimony, illustrations, and other dynamics to help generate a hoped-for conviction of what is being taught. But what about the fifth step of application? How many of the subjects we teach on Sunday are adaptive to this final test of the learning process? Can we only hope that lessons presented will find expression in performance of the same, for it is the doing that proves that learning has taken place? Certainly we must be alert to the danger that application may become short-circuited because of the sedentary requests of the Sabbath.

There are action limitations in whatever we try to teach on Sunday. We do better when our Sunday lessons are fortified, materialized, and practicalized through the experience of *doing* at another place and time. This is where Scouting becomes a laboratory for priesthood holders.

Scouting has the answer to the difference between two kinds of knowledge: the first, knowledge *of* something, and the second, knowledge *about* something. The difference between the two is that knowledge *of* something is learned through personal, direct, firsthand experience, while knowledge *about* something is learned vicariously through instruction, through observation, and through repetition. Both kinds of knowledge are featured in how we learn. Using those definitions we find it easy to assign knowledge *about* something to that which we provide for boys through our efforts in the classroom, specifically in their quorum and Sunday School classes.

Knowledge *of* something comes with the opportunity to perform, to do the thing, or to try to do the thing about which they have learned. Both kinds of knowledge are important! Perhaps boys spend too much time learning *about* things—learning that will enable boys to talk a good story—while their actions may be something quite different. There are many examples of this. A boy may learn about the gospel, but if he does not experience it within himself and internalize it, he may not behave according to its doctrines. Our youth need to learn *about* gospel principles, but they also need to learn *of* them. Thus, for Church leaders it is important to provide means by which boys learn *of* gospel principles by performing them.

Another situation will dramatize how important it is to know *of* something as well as *about* something. As a leader of boys, believing there is a standard of behavior that is important, such as trustworthiness, I should ask myself, *When does a boy become trustworthy? After I have explained it to him? After I have had dialogue with him? After he has repeated it? After he learns how to spell it? After he can respond by word to a definition of it? Has a boy then learned to be trustworthy? Or is there a further test?* I believe so! A boy is not trustworthy until he has had an opportunity to be untrustworthy and has proven that he can be trusted.

I have chosen trustworthiness because it is the first point of the Scout Law. A Scout is trustworthy. It is also a special principle of the gospel. We readily recognize the beauty of helping a boy learn this principle as he gains integrity in the priesthood.

We provide boys with a concept, a leader, and situations under a leader's supervision. Often, by virtue of the leader's foresight and the creation of learning processes, the boy is given an opportunity to prove that he can be trustworthy through performance. When he proves that he can be trustworthy, then there are opportunities for commendation, for loving accolades, and for mutual bonding in which boy and leader together recognize that the boy has performed well. Equally important, if the boy fails then there is the opportunity for the leader to add wholesome support, encouraging the boy to try again, to do better.

I remember a Scoutmaster and a boy emerging from a secluded patch of yellow pine and my meeting with them as I proceeded along the trail in a Scout camp on the North Fork of the Stanislaus River. The Scoutmaster had his arm around the boy as they walked toward me, and I noticed that the boy's cheeks were stained with what seemed to me to be tracks of tears. I wondered about it.

The next day I saw the Scoutmaster, named John Gibson, and I was inquisitive enough to ask, "John, was the boy crying when I met you yesterday on the trail?"

He looked at me for a minute and then said, "Yes, I suppose he had shed a tear or two."

I asked gently, "Would you mind telling me the circumstances?" I was the camp director. It seemed a question I had a right to ask.

He said, "Oh" and chuckled a little bit. "He had found a dollar bill that belonged to one of the other boys in my troop and had not returned it. I had spent a little time with him when we could be alone. It was after we had talked that you met us on the trail." He continued, "I try to find teaching moments. Sometimes they're contrived, but even so they often turn out worthwhile."

John was a great Scoutmaster. He had a waiting list of up to twenty boys wanting to join his troop, which was sponsored by a church in Berkeley. He was adamant about his troop not becoming larger than four patrols.

The following is a quote from Lord Baden-Powell on being a Scoutmaster: "The attitude of the Scoutmaster is of greatest importance, since his boys take their character very much from him; it is incumbent upon him, therefore, to take this wider view of his position than a merely personal one, and to be prepared to sink his own feelings very much for the good of the whole" (*Scouting for Boys* [Ottawa, Canada: The Stores Department, The Boy Scouts' Association], p. 307).

On this issue, President Kimball is quoted under a heading of "Boys Need Heroes Close By": "We are rearing a royal generation—thousands of whom sit with us here tonight—who have special things to do. We need to provide them with special experiences in studying scriptures, in serving their neighbors, and in being contributing and loving members of their families."

President Kimball goes on to quote from Walter MacPeek: "'Boys need lots of heroes like Lincoln and Washington. But they also need to have some heroes close by. They need to know some man of towering strength and basic integrity, personally. *They need to meet them on the street, to hike and camp with them, to see them in close-to-home, everyday, down-to-earth situations; to feel close enough to them to ask questions and to talk things over man-to-man with them.*'" ("Boys Need Heroes Close By," *Ensign,* May 1976, pp. 45, 47; emphasis added.)

5

Help for the Home

Although we stress the leader's role, we recognize that the first and best place for a boy to learn, not only *about* things and *of* things but also in administering or experiencing all five points of the laws of learning, is in the home.

But what if the home is not a model home for boys, a place where all is provided? Many LDS homes do not have as a head of the household a priesthood holder. There are homes where the man is there but is not the man that President Spencer W. Kimball speaks of. The father may even be the one who is in need of more help than the boy. Because of the lack of proper priesthood leadership in the home, we recognize the need for bishops, as presidents of the Aaronic Priesthood, and appointed advisers to become leaders, often surrogate fathers as well as teachers of boys in their ward. These men are crucial in the process of developing successful performance in boys by saying to all boys, "Come, follow me."

Role of the Scouting Program

Two crucial questions are obvious: Who monitors the boy during the other six days of the week to help him perform as he has been taught to perform on Sunday? and Who of our leaders is in the best position to do so?

27

These questions bring into dramatic focus what Scouting is really all about. The bishop must clearly understand why he is forthrightly directed to make certain that his Scouting program, his Scout leaders, and all those that are associated with boys understand what Scouting is supposed to be doing.

This understanding has to focus on the fact that because the Sabbath is filled with no-nos about *doing* and with discussions of gospel principles, Scouting can be a stage, a platform, and a rehearsal period for the performing of spiritual teachings on days in addition to Sunday. This allows us to define a difference between leading and teaching. He who teaches emphasizes the *about* kind of learning, while he who leads seeks opportunities for the *of* kind of learning. When meshed with priesthood objectives, Scouting may add spiritual strength to a boy's character. Scouting values include the mandates of the Scout Oath, with its dramatic and carefully stated concern about doing one's duty to Heavenly Father, country, others, and self. The Scout Oath also provides a daily blueprint of a boy's behavior for all he can experience during the week. In addition, the points of the Scout Law instruct boys to be trustworthy, loyal, helpful, friendly, courteous, kind, obedient, cheerful, thrifty, brave, clean, and reverent. Are those gospel principles? Are these Aaronic Priesthood standards? Of course they are. Those are not outdated virtues; they are, even as measured by the most modern psychiatric yardsticks, solid characteristics of adjustment.

President Karl G. Maeser once said: "I have been asked what I mean by word of honor. I will tell you. Place me behind prison walls—walls of stone ever so high, ever so thick, reaching ever so far into the ground—there is a possibility that in some way or another I may be able to escape; but stand me on the floor and draw a chalk line around me and have me give my word of honor never to cross it. Can I get out of that circle? No, never! I'd die first!" (In *Vital Quotations,* comp. Emerson Roy West [Salt Lake City: Bookcraft, 1968], p. 167.)

The virtues referred to in the Scout Law are also a reaffirmation of the timelessness of honor: "We will never bring disgrace on this, our city, by any act of dishonesty or cowardice. We will fight for the ideals and sacred things of the city" was the code of the boys of

Athens, the Athenian oath, in use five hundred years before the dawn of the Christian era. And today, in the code of Scouting, honor is also important. In one way it is the most important of the Scout laws; it places responsibility upon the boy himself, declaring in effect, "A Scout's honor is to be trusted."

The Scout code says that a Scout does not lie or steal; it says that when a Scout states on his honor that he will do something, he does not need to be watched to make sure that it is carried out. This is the one law that states that a flagrant violator may be asked to turn in his badge. There are rules and responsibilities and consequences of serious import—even in the game of Scouting.

The bishop must hope that those he has called will find a means to influence boys to perform those values. The means for doing those things can come from the Scout meeting, where plans are made that stir the interests found in a boy's world. Those interests carry boys along through the week. If the leader is trained, those plans will be centered in some kind of action. The activities may include the culmination of a skill, a chance to compete, or a chance for social interaction on a boy level, using boy rules, terms, and interests and often planned as a weekend event. This is what Scouting is about!

For the leader, two games are being played: capturing the boy and at the same time helping fashion the boy's behavior. We see the process working as the boy does boy things as the leader is standing near to add encouragement tempered by the constraints associated with the points of the Scout Law and the Scout Oath. Wise leaders cannot be too obvious in why they are really conducting a hike, teaching a boy about the marvels of electricity, or examining the wonders of nature. Nevertheless, keep in mind that paramount to the boy is the fun of Scouting, while paramount to the leader is encouraging the boy to perform wholesomely, thus magnifying his priesthood.

Scouting and Spiritual Growth

It's appropriate to lay at rest what some priesthood brethren have thought to be a negative aspect of Scouting. No one should worry about Scouting being more important than the Aaronic Priesthood in the life of a boy. With maturity, every boy, regardless of his Scouting performance, realizes that Scouting was simply a splendid tool to help him grow into his full magnitude as a priesthood bearer. Scouting helps a boy build integrity for that day when he can experience some of the power and authority promised him through his priesthood commission (see D&C 121:40–46).

Earlier I mentioned that the quorum adviser and Scout leader wears two hats. There is a caution that needs to be expressed, a caution about the two hats. All LDS young men have had one who is commissioned with authority by our Heavenly Father bestow upon him the gift of the Holy Ghost when the young man was confirmed. For most young men reared in the Church, that gift is not pressed into the mind until after a humbling, heart-cleansing experience of the type a convert or even a missionary experiences, a kind of a humbling experience that often fortifies them with deep conviction, thus making application of the gospel much easier.

As a quorum adviser and Scout leader, one may not succeed in presenting the gospel to young men by using only the easier and more formal methods of Sunday-meeting-type practices by teaching only *about* something. One may succeed more completely if the informal kind, teaching *of* something, is not neglected.

6

Why Scout Camping?

It has been proposed that Scouting has an enormous spiritual dimension but that its ability to enhance spiritual values in boys is failing because of faulty leadership perception. For example, if the only chance to teach a boy to be trustworthy is to teach him about being trustworthy, the teaching may end up in the wastebasket of a boy's experience. Trustworthiness is chosen because it is the first point of the Scout Law and is encompassing in its application to a boy's value system more than all other ideals enumerated for Scouting.

Scout camping produces many opportunities to perform acts of being trustworthy. Teaching moments are often produced through camping experiences if those experiences are thrilling and challenging, if they provide high expectations of fun and fellowship and new adventure. Do you announce to a boy that you are going to take a camping trip to teach him to be trustworthy? No, but it may be your objective for a particular camping trip. Many who have had extensive experience with boys know that there are very few activities that provide multiple opportunities for teaching effective values as much as taking a group of boys on a camping trip. Every moment of this kind of experience can, if the leader is alert, expose him and his boys to situations in which there are opportunities to improve behavior patterns.

To emphasize the value of camping experiences in providing opportunities for learning the points of the Scout Law, mentally check them off in terms of involvements and opportunities that will be constantly in front of a boy as he gets involved in all of the direct experiences that are part of a camping trip: trustworthy, loyal, helpful, friendly, courteous, kind, obedient, cheerful, thrifty, brave, clean, reverent.

Parents need to know of the importance of Scout camping. A wholesome Scouting experience for a boy can become very vulnerable if the parent factor is left out of the equation. A confidential dialogue between parents and a leader of boys should reveal the underlying purpose of any camping trip and the purposeful efforts that may be intended by the leader. It should dispel what will be in the mind of many parents as to the underlying purpose of whatever it is that is being planned as an outdoor experience for members of the Scout troop. Such an activity may be publicly announced as a star hike, during which a boy will learn about the universe, or as an overnighter to test the boys' skills in building cooking fires, learning methods of rescue, gaining proficiency in first aid, or any other appeal that catches boys' interest or is required for advancement. But behind all of this, unannounced, is a far more profound purpose which the Scout leader may plan.

The likely expectancy by parents is that the boy will return dirty, sunburned, scratched, or wet, perhaps having caught a cold. However, parents should be aware that there have been other objectives that have been attempted by leadership, objectives which are calculated and designed to help that son of theirs be a better boy. Scouting expects that the rubbing off that will have taken place between wise adult leaders and the boy will have produced a learning experience, one that fits the concept of learning *of* something in addition to *about* something.

This is the finesse of Scouting! In a sense Scouting camouflages a value through an activity with a purpose which the boy has in mind but which may be different from the one the leader has in mind.

An experience that features something of this method, although not directly Scout oriented, happened with my own family. The opportunity presented itself to invite my three older children to accompany me to round up several donkeys that were a feature attraction of a California boys' summer camp. The burros, as usual, had been pastured out for the winter months. With the season upon us to prepare for another summer, we were to round up the burros and haul them up to the High Sierra camp. Scouts would learn to pack their camping gear on their backs for three-day hikes. The burros were located at a ranch near Livermore, California. Our objective included searching for them, rounding them up, and driving them into an enclosed corral. At one end of the corral was a ramp, next to which the stake body truck we were using was placed. This permitted the animals to walk up the ramp and into the truck. All went well until we encountered one burro who was not familiar with the loading process. He was not cooperative. We had a halter on him, and although the children and I added strenuous encouragement we could not get him to come up the ramp. We pulled and we heaved and we coaxed, using Sunday School language. Very little, if any, progress was made. In fact, often we lost ground at every pull. Finally one of the children said, "Dad, let's blindfold him. Maybe we could get him to go up if he can't see." So we grabbed a sweatshirt and tied it around his eyes and head and again put forth our best effort. We still often lost ground. Finally the thought came from one of us, "Let's turn him around, but keep the blindfold on." We turned that old fellow around, keeping the blindfold on. I got behind and put my shoulder to the wheel, his terminal end, while the children pulled on the halter rope. When we stopped suddenly, his wheels being set in reverse allowed us to pick up two or three of his steps backwards. Repeatedly we tried this same trick, heaving and then quickly letting go, and each time we gained a little until the old fellow backed himself in blindfolded obstinacy right up the ramp and into the truck.

I have associated that experience ever since with something similar to what we do with boys. We often blindfold them, in a sense, in Scouting. We sometimes push in one direction with the expectation that boys, being who they are, will move in another direction. It is certain that success is often achieved by getting boys to do things in which values are camouflaged in activities.

7

Scouting in the Primary

Peculiar to the LDS Church is the manner in which Scouting reaches a boy. Its introduction comes from the Primary, and it is important for the Aaronic Priesthood and Scout leader to cooperate with the Primary auxiliary and take advantage of the capable, skilled strength which our Primary personnel offer to the Scouting program. It is noteworthy that the Primary Scout leader—often a woman, sometimes a man and wife—introduces to the prospective Scout the ideals of Scouting—the Oath, Law, slogan, and motto—and completes with the boy all of his Tenderfoot requirements. Some consider this introduction to Scouting the most important part of his Scouting experience, crucial to the success of his progress toward the achievement of Scouting's spiritual impact, his acquisition of the Eagle rank, and his performance of Scouting values throughout his life.

The following thoughts of a new den leader illustrate the concern dedicated Primary leaders feel: "When I was a brand new den leader, I had many questions about the purpose of a den meeting. I started asking other leaders and got these answers: For fun! For advancement. To teach new skills and broaden their horizons. But I didn't feel they quite hit the nail on the head. It wasn't until I was no longer a den leader that I found the secret. But it shouldn't be a secret. I'll share it with you. Character development, citizenship training, personal fitness (inside and out). This is why we do it. I felt I did a good job as a den leader, but I am sorry for all the teaching moments I missed, for all the insight I could have given, for all the pats on the back, words of wisdom, feelings of unity and the list goes on." (Jan Barker, Vice President of Cub Scouting, Utah National Parks Council, in "Do It for the Boy," *Council News,* Winter 1995, p. 6.)

The reader should not conclude that the Primary's intrusion into the standard procedures of Scouting compromises a boy's beginning experience. LDS Scouting becomes vulnerable in its very beginning only when the Primary Scout leader has not been trained to promote a careful relationship with the deacons quorum adviser and Scout leader. Both are to take direction from each other as they teach the meaning of and monitor the practice of the ideals of Scouting, conduct the Scout's investiture ceremony, and secure a skilled performance of Tenderfoot requirements for each boy's first rank as a Scout. We add that our worthy Primary leaders provide a beginning welcome to Scouting that reaches beyond the boys' achievement of worthy behavior and the Eagle rank and adds the sustaining influence Scouting will have to produce missionary performance, temple marriage, and eternal life.

With the announcement for LDS Scouters that women were to become Guide Scout leaders, I was certain that there were disturbances in many areas where Scoutmasters were turning over in their graves. But I assure you that a woman's introduction to our Scouting program was totally appropriate. To ask these wonderful mothers to introduce a boy to Scouting, particularly the ideals of Scouting, was to me significant of the revelatory nature of Scouting's marriage to the Young Men program of the Church. One must not presume to identify that women usurp the practice of priesthood direction for a boy, and one must admit that they do not worry about protocol for they are not timid in pursuing those procedures that get the job done. To the contrary, who better than they to teach boys to sing about Scouting and lift their voices in singing favorite Church hymns while traveling and while camping. Boys in song are the happiest of groups, and in addition to lyrics that typically rehearse poetic fun for boys, their singing can become spiritually impressive. No one can listen to them sing "On My Honor" (Henry Bartlet in *Boy Scout Songbook* 1970, p. 63) or "Called to Serve" (*Hymns,* no. 249) without recognizing a refinement of the soul which thus takes place. May the Lord bless our women to help boys to sing joyously and with fervor.

The concept that carefully marries Scouting to religion, particularly to the quorum efforts of the LDS Church, is valid. Lest there be some thought that it is prostituting the purposes of Scouting to join it with priesthood values and thus use it for a purpose it was not intended for, please note the words of Lord Baden-Powell, the founder of Scouting. He said: "There is no religious *side* to the Movement. The *whole* of it is based on religion, that is, on the realisation and service of God."

Toward the end of his life, Lord Baden-Powell stated: "Let us, therefore, in training our Scouts, keep the higher aims in the forefront, not let ourselves get too absorbed in the steps. Don't let the technical outweigh the moral. Field efficiency, backwoodsmanship, camping, hiking, good turns, jamboree comradeship are all means, not the end. The end is *character*—character with a purpose."

In another quotation we find these words: "Our objective in the Scout Movement is to give such help as we can in bringing about God's Kingdom on earth by inculcating among youth the spirit and the daily practice in their lives of unselfish goodwill and co-operation." (Excerpts from Lord Baden-Powell from personal notes in author's possession.)

8

Special Help for Quorums

It is important to recognize why Scouting can be given such a valuable role in the development of boys within the quorums of the Church. As we examine the operation of the quorum, it becomes apparent that Scouting can provide enormous strength in reaching out and helping accomplish many objectives of the Aaronic Priesthood. Because of its peculiar abilities and strengths, when added to the quorum Scouting acts as a catalyst to help the quorum perform its objectives. Please consider carefully the following:

1. *The quorum can and should become significant and influential in a boy's life if it becomes a peer group.* It should be the most important peer group for LDS boys. Peer influence has proven to be significant; some studies even say all-significant in terms of behavior patterns for boys. How can Scouting help? Scouting helps because Scouting adds adventure to quorum programs. Boys become close friends through the sharing of exciting experiences. It becomes enjoyable when it provides activities that bind boys together. It offers a medium which features characteristics of fun, challenge, and excitement, all of which are bonding agents that grant a peer group the all-important special and exclusive status.

In a peer group, boys do not seek fellowship one with another to satisfy interests that are thrust upon them by adults. In many ways, without Scouting the quorum fits into this category. Effective peer groups form out of mutual boy interests, and often they are the doing kinds of things or the doing kinds of interests in which adults find it hard to give wholesome input. This first catalyst, as with others to follow, identifies that some of our quorums may not have followed the injunction of our priesthood brethren and our General Authorities inviting the combination of quorum adviser and Scout leader. Scouting is designed to automatically bring strength to the quorums through trained Scout leadership.

2. *Quorums can be strengthened if they provide activity with a purpose.* It is not happenstance that in its effectiveness Scouting meets the quorum's needs so nicely, because Scouting is a laboratory. Leaders should know that activities that are planned just for the sake of having an activity may waste time. When the Scout leader is trained to help boys plan activities with purpose, then it can become a laboratory—whether the Scout recognizes it or not—where the worthy purpose, though it may be camouflaged, may be fulfilled.

3. *Quorums can be strengthened and boys within quorums individually can become stronger if they provide for themselves training and learning which they initiate.* Scouting assists by encouraging quorum members to choose wholesome *individual* activities using their own initiative. It provides satisfying rewards for their achievement, awards which become immediate, visible, and recognizable. Scouting appeals to a boy's ego. Although some achievements and awards are not spiritual in one sense, the earning of some badges, for example, is still a very worthy effort. With his Scout books, skilled friends, and family, particularly mother and father, a Scout can perform many achievements on his own and get recognition without being dependent on others.

4. *Quorum programs are better and provide strength for every boy if they are designed and conducted so that the individual interests of a boy are accommodated.* Scouting is organized to require leadership that helps an Aaronic Priesthood boy find an outlet for every interest he may have. He need not be outdoor-minded to be caught up in Scouting. Although camping is a great tool to help in much of what Scouting can provide, some boys are not outdoor-oriented. The program is flexible, and wise Scout leadership can accommodate even the uncommon interests of individuals. The leader

must become intimately acquainted with each boy's interests and needs and become helpful in promoting achievement, regardless of what a boy's special interests are. In Scouting, there are approximately 120 different areas of special interest, and there are challenges for boys in every field of endeavor. Interests can often be expanded by good merit-badge counselors, who can influence Aaronic Priesthood boys in wholesome ways. This includes ways that stir the intellect and provide for the boy an abiding involvement in learning, achieving, and doing things that ignore the outdoors but fascinate him.

5. *It's fun to be in a quorum.* Is it? Well, it should be! Quorums ought to be fun. There are other things that a quorum ought to be also, some of them very profound. But if the quorum provides pleasure and fun, then it has an opportunity to become an even stronger factor in the lives of boys. Scouting adds another dimension to performance requirements of the gospel by featuring game learning. Lord Baden-Powell said, "Had we called it what it was, a society for the promulgation of moral attributes, the boy would not exactly have rushed for it." He was wise enough to announce, at least as far as boys were concerned, that Scouting was a game. To the leader, as we have implied, it is something else, far more than a game.

6. *Quorums help a boy apply gospel principles.* Because Scouting is built around activities that emphasize doing, it helps priesthood holders practice and demonstrate priesthood values. Priesthood and Scout leadership can more effectively step in and add compliments when deserved and discouragement for poor performance. It does not stop with lesson presentation in the classroom. Activity opportunities to train for appreciation of gospel principles are basic to the purpose of the Scout program. A wise saying pronounces, "What I hear, I forget. What I see, I remember. What I do, I know." Scouting, as President Spencer W. Kimball has encouraged us, is doing. "Do it!" he says.

7. *One of the challenges peculiar to goals of the Aaronic Priesthood is that many of them do not provide immediate accomplishment.* Their goals are long-term; they are very profound. The rewards are announced, but they sometimes are to come in the next world. This, of course, is not bad; this is wonderful. However, there is another feature important in terms of goals for boys in the Aaronic

Priesthood. There should be boy-oriented goals that are short-term, accomplishable, and worthy of immediate recognition. Scouting is designed to achieve those very goals. Good performance by a boy expands his character and his influence while he is a boy. Mixed with the achievement and honors, Scouting's codes of conduct complement those proposed by the Savior. These codes are, in a sense, the Beatitudes, the Decalogue, and the Articles of Faith, written in the language of boys. They are goals that provide a boy with an inviting access to the Comforter and his influence.

8. *A strength for quorums is to provide opportunities for Aaronic Priesthood boys to teach the gospel to themselves as well as others.* This duty is described officially in the Doctrine and Covenants as "to teach, expound, exhort" (D&C 20:42). It was a serious challenge given to holders of the Aaronic Priesthood, who at the time were adults. Such words are not likely to excite the interest of many boys. Scouting gives boys an opportunity to teach by example in all types of situations and build the kingdom of God on the earth on weekdays as well as on Sunday. This is the purpose of Scouting according to its founder, and it offers more appeal. This means that every Scout should encourage his friends to become Scouts, if not in his group then in another quorum which has Scouting. What a great opportunity is available for a boy to teach by example, friendship, and encouragement and by being a model of the gospel. This is a special invitation, one which can be very exciting and satisfying. Boys can see themselves as being very special when they can teach the gospel by using Scouting as a means to provide them with opportunities to model the gospel for others. What an exciting and practical challenge is thus provided. It is recognized that it is not easy to invite a non-LDS boy to come into the quorum meeting on Sunday or to be actively engaged therein. To provide the rubbing-off opportunities that Scouting can provide is another matter. Every boy in the quorum automatically becomes a missionary through the performance of good Scouting, if the Scout troop or the Cub pack or any of the Scouting units has been able to encourage the interest of boys who are not LDS. Latter-day Saint parents should recognize and encourage this great opportunity for their boys. It is excellent training for future missionaries.

9. *Quorums should give community service.* Service is a featured quality of quorum practice and behavior. Scouting magnifies the practice of service to others. It invites LDS priesthood boys and leaders into full fellowship with the world's most honored movement for boys in performing service to others. It invites them to become active partners with others in the community in demonstrating good- will and service. We cannot perform the second of the two greatest commandments or spread the gospel by sitting in supposed perfection in our chapels. The Savior said in Mormon 9:22, "Go ye into all the world," and certainly he had service in mind. That charge sends a message to those who are in the quorums: to serve beyond those within the Church is a magnificent challenge for boys. Sorrow, tragedy, and the need of help by others are a blessed invitation to quorum members. The very beginning motto for a Scout, to do one's best, is supported by the motto, "Do a good turn daily." We begin earlier to condition a boy to be helpful to others if Mom and Dad remind him to do a good turn daily. In doing a good turn daily, he becomes a better deacon.

10. *The quorum advisers can become more effective if they become heroes for boys.* Countless men have attained the status of hero because they have become good Scoutmasters. This is not to demean the position of the quorum adviser. It simply means that the Scout leader is provided with opportunities that are not usually available to the quorum adviser unless his work is combined with that of Scout leader. Scouting provides the opportunity to help an adviser become a hero-type in the eyes of his boys. As quorum adviser and Scout leader, he makes it possible for them to have thrilling experiences and challenging accomplishments through Scout activities. He becomes carefully acquainted with each boy through intimate involvements and the sharing of problems. Have you heard a boy refer in worshipful terms to "my" Scoutmaster? Just recently it was my privilege to be listening in on a conversation between boys, one of whom was repeatedly using the phrase *my Scoutmaster.* I caught him as he was leaving a locker room where this had been taking place, and I said, "You talked about 'my Scoutmaster' to your friends a moment ago. Was he a good man?" The boy said with enthusiasm, "Oh yes, he was great." I continued, "Was he also your quorum adviser?" He said, "Oh yes! He was."

It is interesting that in discussions with boys the phrase often used is *my Scoutmaster.* This speaks volumes about a boy's world and things that stimulate them. Heroes are usually doers, and boys are naturally hero worshipers. Quorum advisers have a chance to enrich their assignment by the doing of Scouting and thus to become heroes in the eyes of boys. They must understand that Scouting is a factor that creates hero worship among boys.

11. *Quorum presidencies need to give more than Sunday leadership if the quorum is to be strengthened.* Scouting is organized to invite leadership performances from quorum presidencies if they have accepted the role of leadership of the Scout unit. Neither the adviser nor the elected or appointed leaders can shirk the responsibilities of leadership, of actually performing effectively, when active Scouting is taking place. It is a given that when camping is conducted, for example, more leadership and followership situations will occur than in a whole year of weekly meetings on a Sunday morning. For Scouting, the need for boy leadership is built in, required, and absolutely necessary if Scouting's purposes are to be achieved. When a quorum adviser is Scout trained, this added dimension of leadership experience for quorum members is enormous.

9

Scouting and the Comforter

We have examined some factors that, when exercised by quorums and Scout units, will provide strength to quorum members and help them achieve Aaronic Priesthood objectives. It is the quorum, through its recognized priesthood representation, however, through which all gospel functions should be channeled. This concept only emphasizes how encompassing the priesthood must be. It must shelter everything that prompts the wholesome development and eternal progress of every priesthood holder. Unfortunately, some of us, in giving leadership to the concept of the preeminence of one's priesthood, have neglected to use the spiritual development that Scouting offers to a boy. When a boy is baptized and confirmed, he is given the promise of the gift of the Comforter for spiritual development. Later, when he is ordained to the Aaronic Priesthood, he is granted the power and authority of the priesthood. Spiritually, however, the door may be only unlocked. But more is needed than having someone with authority unlock the door. The boy must help open the door to this special opportunity. Scouting added to the Aaronic Priesthood helps a boy open the door. How is this so?

A basic purpose of blending Scouting into the Aaronic Priesthood is to help the priesthood and Scout leader find and create those teaching moments which will provide a major opportunity for spiritual development. Personal honor, the foundation ideal of Scouting, is a special key to spiritual development. Every priesthood and Scout leader must clearly understand that his major Scout leadership function is to help a boy experience the building of personal honor. All else in Scouting is hinged to this effort. When a boy is first introduced to Scouting, he is introduced to three words which are intended to support all of his Scouting experience. It is hoped that these three words will forever after as long as he lives become a guiding standard for his relationships to any and all others. These words are "On my honor." They are the beginning commitment found in the first part of the Scout Oath. Scouting encourages a boy to exercise personal honor through accepting personal responsibility for his actions.

Through the Scout Oath and its application to the Scout Law, Scouting asks for a personal commitment to establish an internalized accounting book, a book which only the boy can keep. The deacon, teacher, or priest learns to understand that in being a Scout he must have personal honor as a standard of behavior that is his own, under all circumstances and conditions. It is his pact with himself to accept the responsibility of being a son of God. It becomes his method of inviting the Savior to know him personally. Duty to God and country, to others, and to self as found in the Scout Oath and obeying the Scout Law on one's honor are basic entries in this self-internalized account book. To take pride in following those guidelines and to be trusted by others to do so is a foremost step in obtaining power in the priesthood and the promise of the gift of the Comforter.

The word *covenant* comes to mind when one considers personal honor. There is a solemn obligation associated with the word *covenant*, and it is surely one that those who have moved into Melchizedek Priesthood leadership positions are familiar with. In the instance of the Scout Oath and a boy's statement that on his honor he will do certain things, is he not making a covenant with himself? Next to a covenant he might make with his Heavenly Father, could there be anyone else more important with whom he might make a covenant?

A classroom setting at BYU many years ago provided a vivid example of personal honor. The venue was a class being conducted for a course called "Applying Gospel Principles through Youth Programs of the Church." There were forty students involved, both male and female. The discussion featured the principle of honesty. It occurred to me that it might be appropriate to test each other's honesty. The students were invited to stand up and look back into their lives. If they had been entirely honest in the things that they had done, they were to remain standing. On the other hand, if their conscience provoked an almost-forgotten incident of dishonesty, they were to sit down.

After a moment, students began to sit down until finally, including myself, forty of us were sitting down. Only one was standing. The young man who was standing was Larry Echohawk, a future attorney general for the state of Idaho and member of the Brigham Young University Law School faculty. He had played defensive end for BYU during the fall semester of his last year on the football team. I remember watching him. The single wing formation was popular during that time period in our football team's development. Time after time, opposing teams ran a play called an end around, in which the man carrying the ball was preceded by a number of blockers.

Larry Echohawk was often called upon to meet that play. Time after time, in what seemed to me a glorious display of bravery, he withstood the attack of the blockers and the ballcarrier and more often than not stopped the play with little or no gain. I thought of him then as being very brave, which is the tenth point of the Scout Law.

Larry Echohawk was the only one left standing in that class of forty-one, including myself, all of whom were looking intently at him. Rather than dramatize the situation to his embarrassment, I quickly said, "Larry, it is splendid to see this. Will you tell us why it is that you have come this far in life and are reporting that you have been careful not to take something that didn't belong to you?" Without hesitation and without displaying a sense of importance directed toward self-aggrandizement—although I think bravery was being displayed—he simply said, "Brother, the reason is, I am Larry Echohawk." With that, he sat down. A lively discussion followed. But the point was made, and forty of us in that classroom had been introduced to a new appreciation of what it means to make a covenant with one's self.

It cannot be emphasized enough that personal honor is a key to spiritual development. Every priesthood and Scout leader must clearly understand that his major and foremost Scout adult leadership function is to help a boy build a sense of personal honor, and all else in Scouting should directly or indirectly be aimed at teaching this principle. The teaching of such sensitive things, spiritual things, often can best be done gradually. To be trustworthy, to do what one has promised to do and is expected to do, is the essence of personal honor. When a priesthood and Scout leader conducts an activity, he provides a laboratory to help a boy practice and apply behavior patterns. The boy and his peers may give measurement to the kind of honor they possess as they respond to the challenges found in the behavior guidelines of the Scout Oath, Law, motto, and slogan. Leaders must not forget that those activities are to be exciting, fun-filled, and with purpose. Those activities must be adventuresome, demanding skills that are challenging and developmental. They must fit the fifth step of the learning process: application.

Surrogate Fathers and Scouting

An adviser and Scout leader must in truth be to boys all the things that a bishop would want to be, if he could. There is no other assignment, other than that of bishop, that is more important to our young men of the Church than that of quorum adviser and Scout leader.

There is a reason this assignment, which invites boys to follow you, is so important. It is one which identifies why your calling is so wonderful. You do, in truth, become a second father to your boys, without some of the problems that most dads face. A boy is trying to grow up, trying to be as big and independent and important as his dad. As he gets older, of teacher and priest age, he wants to learn to fly on his own, and many dads lose the enormous influence they had earlier, when their boys were younger.

I have personally heard advisers and Scout leaders make the observation, "These are my boys," and they mean it. "I know them better than their parents!" They do in many ways. Boys can talk to advisers and Scout leaders and will follow them when leaders show personal interest, love, and understanding. These leaders become effective surrogate fathers.

Here are some quotes from former students of mine who found advisers and Scout leaders helping out sometimes when dads were finding it tough going with their sons: "He was at all times a friend." "He took a special interest in me." "He was one of us, one who would talk with me, one who always had time for me." "We had fun together." "He cried and he laughed with us." "We knew he was hurt when we could have done better." "We always knew he expected us to do our best, but he didn't scold." "He liked us; he liked to do things we liked to do." "He would listen to our problems." "He took time to help me." "He didn't preach to us." "He was glad to have us come around." "His wife was great. We loved her."

The preceding reasons are why, all over the Church, men are being released from what we have considered positions of supreme importance and shifted to become boys' leaders if they have skills that can interest boys and do things boys like to do. The Church must never be just a Sunday, go-to-meeting assignment for boys. This is also why we are calling back into active youth leadership former stake presidents, high councilmen, and members of bishoprics who have proved they know boys and enjoy being part of their world.

The reference previously made to the role that the Scoutmaster and quorum adviser plays in helping boys and performing in an assistant, but effective, fatherly role is reinforced by some pronouncements made by President David O. McKay in a speech delivered to the faculty of Brigham Young University on September 18, 1953. "In reality, the teacher, instead of being merely an ally, must become the foster parent in training the child in the art of living. If that were all, his responsibility would be great enough. It is not all. Often he faces even the greater task of overcoming false teaching and the vicious training of unwise, irresponsible parents." (*Excerpts from Speech by President David O. McKay to faculty at Brigham Young University,* September 18, 1953. Copy in author's possession.)

10

It's the Doing That Counts

Remember the reference to brevity made earlier wherein it was suggested that in working with boys, the quorum adviser and Scout leader is encouraged to avoid extended dialogue or speech-making situations where he expounds at great length while youth hopefully listen. Perhaps such teaching and learning, if it is to take place, is better handled in the classroom or in situations in which sedentary behavior is expected. In contrast, the tool that the quorum adviser and Scout leader uses when he is featuring Scout training or Scouting activity is one that focuses on the doing rather than on lecture and discussion. The Scout laws, as published by the Boy Scouts of America, dutifully reflect this concept. It would be appropriate to examine each point of the Scout Law in terms of the explanation that is offered. Parenthetically, I do not subscribe to the instruction that the eleven-year-old Scout, when earning his Tenderfoot requirements, be asked to repeat only the twelve points of the Scout Law. The explanations of each are of supreme meaning and should be memorized by each boy. The twelve points of the Scout Law and an explanation of each follow:

> *A Scout is trustworthy.* A Scout tells the truth. He keeps his promises. Honesty is a part of his code of conduct. People can always depend on him.

A Scout is loyal. A Scout is true to his family, friends, Scout leaders, school, nation, and world community.

A Scout is helpful. A Scout is concerned about other people. He willingly volunteers to help others without expecting payment or reward.

A Scout is friendly. A Scout is a friend to all. He is a brother to other Scouts and all the people of the world. . . .

A Scout is courteous. A Scout is polite to everyone, regardless of age or position. He knows that good manners make it easier for people to get along together.

A Scout is kind. A Scout understands there is strength in being gentle. He treats others as he wants to be treated. Without good reason, he does not harm or kill any living thing.

A Scout is obedient. A Scout follows the rules of his family, school, religion, and troop. He obeys the laws of his community. . . .

A Scout is cheerful. A Scout looks for the bright side of life. He cheerfully does tasks that come his way. He tries to make others happy.

A Scout is thrifty. A Scout works to pay his own way [if I were his leader, I would add "and helps pay for his mission"] and to help others. He protects and conserves natural resources. He carefully uses time and property.

A Scout is brave. A Scout can face danger even if he is afraid. He has the courage to stand for what he thinks is right even if others laugh at him or threaten him.

A Scout is clean. A Scout keeps his body and mind fit and clean. He chooses the company of those who live by these same ideals. He keeps his home and community clean.

A Scout is reverent. A Scout is reverent toward God. He is faithful in his religious duties. He respects the beliefs of others. (*The Boy Scout Handbook* [Irving, Texas: Boy Scouts of America, 1990], pp. 553–61.)

It is obvious that the leader, in presenting the principles enunciated as the points of the Scout Law, is encouraged not to expound too much about them. Rather the encouragement is to seek out opportunities in which behavioral patterns can be observed and praise voiced. Also, it is a leader's opportunity to register disappointment when the boy in his activities violates the ideals which he has promised on his honor to uphold.

President Gordon B. Hinckley provided a penetrating observation about the significance of the Scout motto, "Be prepared," at a historic meeting to mark the 75th Diamond Jubilee of the Boy Scouts of America in 1985. The idea of living and doing is one of tying knots that will hold under pressure, he said. Poorly tied knots "are evident in career failures, in business failures, in professional failures, in marriage failures. To be able to tie the right knot for the right reason, for the right occasion, and to have it hold against every stress is part of the process of being prepared." (See Kevin Stoker, "Mighty Results Flow from Scout Program," *Church News*, 17 February 1985, pp. 3, 11.)

Meetings—Square Pegs in Round Holes

An example of a boy's rejection of the use of extended dialogue in a Church meeting occurred in a ward chapel in New Zealand filled mostly by adults listening to a relay of a general conference. President Thomas S. Monson delivered a powerful message. Everyone in attendance seemed pleased, it appeared.

Not true for the boy sitting next to me. As soon as conference ended, he immediately sprang into action and politely but swiftly moved to the aisle, almost climbing over those sitting next to him. As an apology for his actions, he said, "Let me out! I've had it up to here!" Sitting for two hours on a hard bench listening to conference talks, regardless of how good they are in the opinion of adults, is not exactly a come-on for boys of Scout age.

The point is further supported by a study conducted by the Youth Leadership department of Brigham Young University in which a sampling was taken of over two thousand LDS boys randomly selected from wards and stakes positioned in every part of our nation. These boys, ages fourteen to eighteen, reported that of the ten options of things they enjoyed doing, the one that suggested religious activity, such as going to church, always came in last (Thane J. Packer, "Interests and Values of Latter-day Saint Adolescent Males," Salt Lake City: University of Utah, 1974.) We are fortunate that we get a portion of our boys to accept our formats that feature sitting and listening for long periods of time—long periods in terms of boys' estimates. The same preference was demonstrated by boys of other faiths in a similar study by Yankolovich, Associates.

The disinterest in the classroom setting featuring sedentary participation by our youth is universal for the Church. Regardless of race or culture, our boys are like most boys. Let me take you to an incident occurring in Guadalajara, Mexico, to support this view. The setting was a combined quorum meeting of the Aaronic Priesthood groups, with about fifteen boys attending. After priesthood meeting came Sunday School. The Sunday School class roll showed only two boys in class. Not wishing to interrupt or disturb the teacher and the lesson, I discreetly asked the priesthood class teacher about what had happened to the boys. His response was unforgettable. "Oh, about an hour is all we can expect. I think you'll find them down the street a ways."

My curiosity prompted my looking for them outside the chapel. They were gathered around a hot-rod vehicle. It was parked on a nearby street. The vehicle, being unusual, generated dreams of special excitement and performance for each boy, who as he admired it probably wished that he might someday own one like it.

The boys had, I suspect, no conscientious thought of the greater, far-reaching time value had they remained in the Sunday School class with its concern about things that were far more spiritual and worthy of special excitement for each of these holders of the Aaronic Priesthood. These were Latter-day Saint Mexican boys, and it is likely that there was little difference in their interests from other boys their age, regardless of race or religious preference.

11

Not Only on the Sabbath

Another reference will further illuminate the limitations of using Sunday meetings as a singular method of helping the gospel come alive in the hearts and souls of our boys. While I was on a special assignment to New Zealand, the bishop of a local ward told me that of the ten priests that were on the records for this ward, none were active. All ten were doing other things on Sunday. One of the ten happened to be an acquaintance of mine. No details of the ward's effort to activate him were presented, but the response of the bishop, which seemed to express the adult mind-set of many leaders about the appeal of Church meetings for boys, was forthright and matter-of-fact. It was a dismissal by way of righteous intent. The response was, "You know, we just have never been able to get that boy to come to church." A similar situation likely prevailed for the other nine, since all ten were inactive. Like the boy who had sat next to me during the conference broadcast, they had also probably had it up to here. I later learned that except for an oasis of Aaronic Priesthood performance in a few selected wards, almost universally the activity of the priest quorums in New Zealand was somewhat a mirror of the inactivity of those boys.

An exception to such failure was largely generated by John Kendall, a Scout leader commissioned by the Scout Association of New Zealand as the national chaplain for all LDS groups. Under his direction, the Aaronic Priesthood performances were very good in his stake. They embraced a vigorous Scout program and an encompassing vision of how and what was necessary to enlist the broad interests of boys. John Kendall's story dramatizes the cautionary wisdom and the challenge of self-sacrifice that face the youth of the Church concerning Sunday involvement. John described on more than one occasion by piecemeal referral the evolution of himself to becoming an active member of the Church and a great Aaronic Priesthood and Scout leader. These occasions included the wisdom of a mother who did not insist that John exclude his interest in soccer on Sunday.

Activating the Youth

At another time and in another setting, it was the priesthood meeting of a ward in Tahiti that produced further insight into boys and their natural aversion to Sunday meetings. The occasion drew from me great disappointment for our Aaronic Priesthood efforts and an enormous sympathy for boys, who were obviously suffering during their attendance at this portion of their Sunday experience. The room was small, not more than ten-by-twelve feet, with a desk taking up some of the room and with a lesson being read verbatim from the lesson manual by an unskilled reader. The room was crowded with boys, some sitting on the floor for lack of chairs, some standing against the wall, and some sitting partially in one windowsill. Those boys were there because of the gentle, long-suffering nature of the Polynesian race, but nonetheless they were suffering physically. No one, it seemed, was listening. This was their regular formal priesthood exposure! The temperature was typically Tahitian, which means it was very warm and muggy; all were greatly perspiring. One can fully understand and not be surprised that the boys, as they became priests, found more inviting things to do than go to church on Sunday. The high incidence of inactivity and the avoidance of missionary experiences as they became of age was common, not the exception.

Trained adult Scout leadership provides vitality to the quorum. Proper training provides skills in performing and doing before boys, with boys, and among boys, and it reserves the preachment practices, which are often too easily performed, for classroom-type settings or sedentary situations. An impressive reference is found in the Boy Scout manual published by the Scout Association of New Zealand referring to the Scoutmaster's Minute. Scouting uses the suggestion of the Scoutmaster's Minute as a time when it becomes appropriate to preach of values and standards. Hopefully, it is when boys are listening intently—a moment chosen by the leader that will provide the opportunities for impressive listening. In a caution provided in a Scouting manual published some fifty years ago is this rather bold statement that should apply now also: "If a Scoutmaster spends more than three or four minutes in performing or presenting a Scoutmaster's Minute to boys, he ought to be shot." Oftentimes we are prone to expound at great length to boys on subjects better handled with brevity and by choosing sensitive situations and impressive conditions.

Outdoor Sunday Services

It is appropriate to make some observations about the keeping of the Sabbath day, as it may be challenged by traditional activities conducted by some Scout associations. Not all religious sponsors of Scouting are locked into or emphasize the significance of attending church meetings on Sunday, but rather some find it advantageous to perform in other special ways. Many Scout associations will schedule the observance of national holidays to include the convenience of Sunday in their calendar of activities. LDS leaders in other countries often run into this situation and find it very awkward. However, with careful dialogue between LDS and non-LDS Scout leaders, an occasional and acceptable LDS participation can be forthcoming. An example is the arrangements nicely worked out by the Boy Scouts of America for events such as a national or world jamboree. An event of a very special nature, possibly on a district level or even ward level, sometimes may be planned for a Sunday. The overriding issue in this situation is the great advantage that can come to a quorum adviser and Scout leader and the bishop to hold a Sunday outdoor service of their own in which only the bishop, or proper authority, and the boys are participating. An example of an appropriate outdoor worship service is one held for the commemoration of the restoration of the Aaronic Priesthood. Positive experiences have occurred in which the bishop and his advisers and Scout leaders have deliberately planned a weekend adventure that includes a Sunday dedicated to the meaning and significance of the restoration of the Aaronic Priesthood. This can be viewed as appropriate because the actual events of this memorable occasion took place in the out-of-doors on the banks of the Susquehanna River.

It has also been the experience of many that when testimony meetings are held in the outdoors, with all of the advantages that can be associated in meeting within the creative atmosphere of our Heavenly Father, the performance of boys is remarkable. Perhaps you have had the experience when, in a situation of this kind, every boy will stand and bear his testimony. Often the performance of boys in testimony meeting in chapel settings is disappointing. In company with all ages of Church membership, boys will rarely actively perform, whereas among themselves and especially in the outdoors with the "Come, follow me" example practiced by a bishop and leaders, every boy will perform in remarkable ways and find it satisfying to do so. Preserved and remembered by many are those most precious experiences in which groups of boys have banded together on a Sabbath morning to individually bear their testimonies, many for the first time in their lives.

Special recollection of this for me comes from an event developed as a part of an observance by the Scouts of New Zealand. It was a district activity planned as part of a national holiday. With permission granted by a stake president, one of his wards was participating in a weekend commemorating the founding of New Zealand. Knowing the importance of meeting together in a Scout's Own, a New Zealand Scout term for Sunday worship, this LDS group was given the privilege of using the camp's worship facility. Delegation for directing this Scout's Own was awarded to the leader of the priests group. Bright in my memory is the performance of one young man who, after having supervised the administration of the sacrament, stood up wearing his new uniform and spoke of the sacrifice of its purchase and how it represented to him many things, not the least of which were duty to God, others, and self and the Scout Law,

motto, and slogan. He also expressed his gratitude to his parents, his
love of the Savior, and his testimony of the truth of the Church.
Strikingly, before he sat down he included the direct invitation for
his assistant in the quorum to take his place. The assistant responded,
as did each boy in turn. Having run through the entire membership
of the priests quorum, the presidency of the teachers and then the
deacons offered a similar invitation to each boy to stand and bear
testimony. It was rewarding because all the boys contributed to that
very spiritual event. There was the temptation to compare it to what
might have happened in the routine of the usual Sunday meeting of
the quorum which would have occurred in the ward had they remained at home on that Sunday.

Another personal experience involved a training course dedicated
by title to the spiritual values of Scouting. It was designed by the
New Zealand Scout Association and held as part of a course for leaders of groups. *Group* was the inclusive term used by that association
to include all the families of Scouting—Cubs, Scouts, and Venturers.
Scout leaders of different faiths attended the course, and as the course
progressed members were divided into a deliberate mixing of faiths.
In the group of reference were five men, including one Catholic, one
Methodist, one Presbyterian, a member of the Church of God, and
myself. The assignment was to gather from nature a representation of
materials and to so design them that they would portray the manger
scene and the birth of the Savior. Can you imagine this diversity of
faiths pooling resources, ideas, and suggestions, cooperating by invitation to put together something of this kind? We performed, in my
estimation, magnificently. The course members were so proud of the
exhibit that they insisted on keeping it assembled throughout the rest
of the day and placing it on exhibit where all course members could
view it. More important was the bonding that developed among the
five of us and the close friendships that were established because of
this opportunity to work together—manually, spiritually, and cre-
atively—in preserving for each the significance of that memorable
event which was basic to each of our faiths.

12

Tragedy of Untrained Scout Leaders

I cannot overemphasize the importance of Scout training for an Aaronic Priesthood leader. Perhaps Scouter training would be more accurate because it clarifies the essentiality of this involvement. If any man called by a bishop to lead Scouting is to succeed, Scout training is preeminently necessary, particularly for the LDS man. This training is necessary because his primary qualifying experience for accepting a Church calling has often come by a general absorption of gospel principles and purposes as he has attended meetings, usually in a sedentary setting. If he is asked by the bishop to serve both as adviser and Scout leader, he can become the "Come, follow me" kind of leader if he becomes Scout trained.

Elder Vaughn J. Featherstone has admonished, "I do not believe that Varsity Scouting is on trial in the Church, nor is Boy Scouting, Cub Scouting, or Exploring. But rather it is my firm belief that bishops, and the ward leaders, the advisers, Scoutmasters, coaches, and Explorer advisers are on trial. The program will work if they will work and become trained and put into effect the things they have been trained to do." He states further:

> There are four things that are absolutely essential in a great scout leader. I call them the four T's:

1. Testimony—that they have a testimony of the Lord Jesus Christ, His atonement, and that this church is God's church.

2. Trained—they need to be trained, not only by the church, but as well by Boy Scouts of America within the districts and council.

3. Time—they need to have time to be a leader of boys.

4. Tenure—short tenure if they don't enjoy the work and are not willing to put in the time necessary, and long tenure if they love the young men and want to serve them with all of their hearts and souls. (From personal letter to author, 7 October 1997.)

The Church has had a long history of inexcusable performance by untrained Scout leaders in which boys have suffered, physical tragedies have occurred, activity experiences have been mediocre at best, and the very purposes of the blending of Scouting into the quorum have been lost completely. The leader has supposed that he could conduct the Scouting concerns of his boys without having been trained to do so.

Sadly, wards have had misconceptions of what Scout leadership should provide. Only in recent years have bishoprics recognized that it is folly and a serious error to use a Scoutmaster calling as a means to try to activate adults who are inactive and who cannot, by virtue of their modeling, represent all that the Church stands for and expects from its leaders. Occasionally we have rescued someone from inactivity through the call to become a Scoutmaster. But on the whole, hundreds and hundreds and maybe thousands of our boys have become sacrificial lambs when this practice has been followed. Such boys have been betrayed in the sense that all the great advantages and opportunities that good Scouting could provide for them have been sacrificed in the hope of bringing a wayward man into activity through the program of Scouting. Experience suggests that if we hope to activate someone through Scouting, the appointment should be one in which the man is not expected to model Scouting for boys. It would be in everyone's best interest for this individual to hold a position as a committee man, something with indirect responsibility, until proven worthy as a role model for our Aaronic Priesthood quorum members and fully and carefully trained in the methods of Scouting.

It is a true Scout axiom that merely good men do not necessarily make good Scout leaders. It is also true that boys ask for more than being faithful in one's religious duties in order for a man to be a successful Scout leader. According to President Ezra Taft Benson:

> Ours is not a boy problem; it is a man problem. Our boys want Scouting: we want them to have it. Our problem is in leadership. Our great need is to provide the leadership to meet the demands of the boys. Through Scouting we can help them develop real character; we can teach them cooperation; we can help them develop qualities of leadership; we can teach them the value of staying power. . . .
>
> Let's mobilize men, hundreds of them, who love boys; who believe in them; who not only have the technical skills, but who will inspire them, because boys need inspiration even more than they need information. Boys are hero-worshipers; they are great idealists; they love to follow one whom they regard as their ideal, their pal, their champion! (*God, Family, Country: Our Three Great Loyalties* [Salt Lake City: Deseret Book, 1974], pp. 214–15.)

Past events in the story of our Scouting efforts with boys document the vital need to call to those positions men who have special talents that can be transferred so as to stimulate Church interests in boys. This was clearly demonstrated in the 1960s before the MIA was dissolved. It was then that a set of objectives was announced for all quorums of the Church to examine as measurements of performance. Certificates of recognition were offered that suggested that if the quorum could meet a set of proposed standards during the course of the year, it could and would be recognized as being one of the top quorums of the Church. Applications were circulated, and annual recognitions were announced during June conference. Priest quorums and Explorer units that performed in a stellar fashion during the year were invited to attend June conference. Included in the invitation was the encouragement to bring to conference a display of an activity which was singularly successful in helping to promote the achievement of standards of quorum excellence. The standards covered a rather complete set of measurements of priesthood purposes, including activation of members, activities designed to prepare and promote interest in missionary service, evidence of observance of the Word of Wisdom, and giving welfare and temporal service, to name a few.

In examining those groups, it was found that without exception each of those priest quorums and Explorer posts had a leader who possessed a special skill of interest to boys of priest age. He was a doer. Of the fifty posts presenting demonstrations at one June conference, every one except six had a leader who was or who had become skilled in the doing of a special activity. Each of the remaining six reported that they had developed a special doing activity through the use of consultant help of other skilled doers. Those priests were reporting and demonstrating that their particular activity had been a catalyst that helped achieve priesthood spiritual objectives. They had become one of the better quorums of the Church. The presented skills covered a broad horizon of special interests that would appeal to boys of this age. Each quorum used men of "towering strength," to quote President Kimball (quoting Walter MacPeek, in "Boys Need Heroes Close By," *Ensign,* May 1976, p. 47), who were saying to boys, "Come, follow me" not only in the lessons that they prepared on Sunday but in living and doing exciting things with boys on the other days of the week.

13

Peer Leadership

I cannot stress enough the importance of adding Scout training to other special qualifications that leadership requires of quorum advisers. Scouter training features how to teach boys to lead other boys. It is so important to have a bishop call a boy who can give exemplary leadership to the quorum, besides on Sunday. Scouter training recognizes that the process of selection, guidance, and use of peer leadership within its group is absolutely fundamental. In the Scout troop, for example, this peer leadership is called the patrol method. In the quorum, priesthood leadership by peers comes through the quorum presidency. It is of extreme importance that these boy priesthood leaders are taught, understand, and accept the role of Scouting within the quorum and that they give leadership to Scouting. Without careful attention to and cultivation of this opportunity, much of that which builds integrity through the priesthood in the mind and heart of every boy can be lost. A chance to perform leadership responsibilities in every situation can be a significant experience, perhaps of paramount importance, as a boy grows into manhood and moves into positions of Melchizedek Priesthood leadership and discipleship.

Whoever said that we must learn how to follow before we can lead stated a profound truth. When both processes are functioning within a quorum coupled with Scouting activities, those learning experiences are fostered. So important was it for leadership functions to be operative among boys that a policy from the Church's Aaronic Priesthood committee mandated that those selected by the bishop to perform as boy leaders of the quorums were also to serve as the leaders of the duplicate Scout units. This directive proved impractical because some quorum presidencies were not equipped to lead both quorums and Scout units at the same time. Lack of Scout training was the main problem for the quorum officer. Later, Church direction was modified to allow for the input of boys' preferences in the selection of the boy leaders for Scout activities. It was eventually given to the boy officer, however selected, to say to those of his peers, "Come, follow me." This invitation encompasses the broad scope of performance before one's peers and extends itself beyond a few minutes of responsibility on Sunday, which sometimes without Scouting was the limit of the leadership performance of boys in our quorums.

The challenge of "Come, follow me" becomes a life challenge, certainly an encompassing one in terms of any kind of participation in which boys give or offer influence and leadership to other boys. Fortunate is the bishop who has within his quorums boys who project influence and worthy leadership beyond the assignments that represent the limited vision of what quorum leadership asks in just a Sunday performance. Once again, in boy leadership for Scout units, as well as in the quorum presidency, training is of significant importance.

A previous paragraph referred to a boy who gave special leadership to others in terms of testimony bearing in a priesthood meeting situation while the boys were at camp. Perhaps the most marvelous of all the interplay of forces that develop between boys is when one or some of the group rise and exercise power in the priesthood. By exhibiting strength, courage, and a recognition of appropriate values, they ask for a better performance or an improved performance from their peers. A book could be written filled with documentations of boys who have said to others in a worthy fashion, "Come, follow me." Often they have rectified the direction being taken by their peers and have charted a better course for them to follow. Certainly the printed explanation for the "brave" point of the Scout Law is one that ought to be memorized by every boy who is introduced to the Aaronic Priesthood and the Scouting program. It says, "A Scout can face danger even if he is afraid. He has the courage to stand for what he thinks is right even if others laugh at him or threaten him." (*The Boy Scout Handbook*, p. 558.) How beautiful is the boy who, in his personal accounting of what honor means, takes literally the importance and the meaning of those words, given as an explanation of how a Scout is brave, how a deacon is brave.

An example of Scout bravery is worthy of note. It is only one in a legion of my experiences. The setting was a conference being held on the campus of Utah State University in Logan, Utah. Boys attending were of Explorer age, sixteen to eighteen. The conference was given the title of "Citizens Now." About three hundred boys gathered from all of the towns located in the Cache Valley area. The boys represented nine stakes and seventy wards. At bedtime, getting boys into their bunks after an active day is always a serious challenge. In this instance curfew had come and gone, and lights had been turned out. The boys were sleeping in a gymnasium-type facility that had been curtained off to form compartments. The boys were grouped by fours in two double bunk beds, the curtains being about head high to provide some semblance of privacy for each group. Deciding to make a quick trip home in order to pick up a forgotten toothbrush, I left the scene. In turning the corner toward home, I looked back towards the building and noticed that the lights were back on. Having had this situation happen before leaving and believing that the boys had finally settled down, this instance of curfew infraction was most irritating. I whirled around in my automobile and screeched to a stop back at the building. As the screech of my brakes announced my arrival, out went the lights again. Wanting to find who the culprits were, I left the car and quietly entered the building. Two sets of swinging doors provided entrance to the large room. The first set would swing closed before the second set was pushed open, thus helping disguise my presence.

All was dark. Some chuckling was coming from the other end of the room. As my eyes adjusted to the darkness, I found that garbage cans were being used as substitutes for bowling balls, the aisles between the bunk beds being the lanes for the bowlers. There was considerable merriment being expressed as those cans came hurtling down the aisles banging against the bunk beds in the semidarkness.

A universal interest was created in such an exaggerated bowling activity. One can ended up very close to where I stood. But suddenly attention was demanded by a voice that said, calling a boy by name, "Give us the poem, give us the poem!" Others, who had apparently heard a rendition of what was being asked for, joined in. After some coaxing, the boy began to repeat a verse couched in poetic language which was very uncomplimentary to the boy and to those who were called upon to listen. The words in the verse were exaggerated evidence that this boy had been exposed to the very filthiest of language and depraved thoughts. As he finished the verse, encouragement came from a buddy to continue, saying, "Give us another one, another verse!" The boy started again.

Now being thoroughly perturbed, I began to move down the aisle to the spot from which was coming this very un-Scoutlike, un-priesthoodlike performance. Silently I prayed all the while, hoping that someone of this group, just some one of this three hundred would voice an objection. Certain it was that everyone in the room was hearing what was being said. Just as I arrived at the spot, my prayers were answered as an objection was generated from the end of the aisle. I could see the vague movement of a boy as he brushed aside the curtains of his bunk and shouted, "I've had enough! Let's stop this right now." In conjunction with this voiced objection, the lights came on, and I could see a boy standing there having reached the battery of switches that were located on the wall next to his bunk. His actions also revealed me standing by the enclosure from which the words were coming from. One had been saying, "Come, follow me" in a very negative and disturbing way, and another shined forth with all the beauty and courage that every boy could be proud of. Certainly one cannot overestimate or even overdramatize opportunities of this kind. Priesthood laboratories provide legions of opportunity to bring impressive forces to bear which repeatedly will produce wholesome results between those who lead and those who follow.

14

To Teach, to Apply, to Govern

A review of reasons Scouting should be fitted into the programs of the quorums is appropriate. Scouting serves beautifully as a catalyst to magnify a boy's spiritual experience as a holder of the Aaronic Priesthood. Its ideals expand and encourage the performance of Aaronic Priesthood purposes. It adds boy appeal to the quorum through action and adventure. It requires unparalled leadership performance from quorum presidencies. It has a binding influence that promotes boys to perform as buddies and as a group as they explore new interests and learn rewarding skills. It is designed to make use of application, which is the most effective of all methods of learning gospel principles. It offers immediate and visible rewards for wholesome achievement—badges and public recognition, which, for boys holding the priesthood, is super.

Scouting can help fight two great battles for the Church in its effort to lift up the family. It does so by adding to the ability of bishops and quorum advisers to put their arms around boys who are less active or who have less-active fathers or who are without fathers. Those leaders can then become important surrogate family members. Secondly, it helps the quorum become a dynamic peer group, thus negating the influence of questionable associates who otherwise influence boys to deviate from performing in accordance to gospel principles.

All boys in our quorums have had the experience of having hands laid upon their heads and commissions of a very profound and extraordinary nature conferred upon them as the gift of the Comforter was promised. It is likely, however, that no outward manifestation occurred or no inward consuming experience developed as is sometimes reported in the scriptures. In most cases, what happened is that those with authority unlocked the door to some very special experiences for the boy when they conferred the right to receive the Comforter. But the boy, in order to have those special experiences, was challenged with the responsibility to open the door. How?

A generic answer would be by participating in all of the special opportunities the gospel affords. Joseph Smith said, "I teach the people correct principles, and they govern themselves" (quoted in John Taylor, *The Gospel Kingdom*, ed. G. Homer Durham [Salt Lake City: Bookcraft, 1964], 323); however, we need to be careful about misinterpreting the word *teach*. The word *govern* is the conclusion of the teaching process. Too often as leaders we assume that to teach, as we have already implied, means to present principles in the classroom setting or as a speech. Some youth leaders unfortunately see that method as their major objective and obligation. The truth is, it is only the beginning. The Prophet said, "Teach . . . correct principles." What he did not say but might have said was that the gospel and the Church uses, above all else, the fifth step of the learning process—application. True, the restored gospel exposes us to new truths. True, the Church provides us with repeated exposure. True, the Church provides us with an extensive array of tools and methods to help us understand. And true, the Lord grants us the blessing of his Holy Spirit to convince us that certain things are true. But the bottom line in the teaching and learning of the gospel are found in the opportunities to apply the gospel. Why was the gathering of Saints so necessary in the early history of the Church? And why do we now gather regularly? So that in support of one another we can practice all of the steps of the learning process, including the most important one: helping each other apply the truths. The Lord gives us opportunities for the doing of the gospel. *No power is available to any of us unless we empower ourselves by doing certain things. Understanding is not enough. Exposure is not enough. Repetition is not enough. Even conviction is not enough. All are precursors of something else: the doing or application of the gospel.* Our meetings on Sunday, our support of one another in fellowship, our socials together, our acceptance of calls to serve in a hundred different ways all identify with that final step of the learning process. It is no accident that the last three Articles of Faith identify the application of our beliefs. Scouting provides a mirror of performance by the Aaronic Priesthood to help validate the Prophet Joseph Smith's observation about teaching correct principles that then sets in motion governance, or the application of the gospel.

15

Special Challenges

Advisers and Scout leaders face some special challenges. Those include getting all quorum members interested in Scouting, getting parents to support special Scout activities, getting boys to give talks in church, getting quorum leaders to function in using boys to encourage gospel behavior in others, building interest for boys in missionary service, and helping boys magnify their priesthood callings. Unfortunately, some situational circumstances produce roadblocks that develop as we offer Scouting's assistance to the quorums. Following are six challenges common to boys in their Aaronic Priesthood experience which Scouting is particularly able to help correct.

First Challenge: Getting Boys Involved

To get boys involved and interested in Scouting, take them camping. There can be significant differences between what happens on a regular camping trip and what happens on a *Scout* camping trip. Just because the leader finds himself comfortable in the outdoors and may have hunted or fished, he may not qualify to take boys Scout camping. Scout training for the quorum adviser and Scout leader is a must before he takes his boys camping. Scout camping is always camping with a purpose. The purpose will be to learn special skills while practicing to live the ideals of Scouting.

Second Challenge: Enlisting Parental Support

Why should parents support Scouting as a priesthood activity? The conversation that follows should be directed to parents and should answer this question. The Scout leader is speaking, and Sister Jones is listening. "Sister Jones, when your boy goes camping, he hopes to have fun. We hope to provide him with that kind of experience. We will also give him many chances to practice living the ideals of Scouting while he camps. One of my most important purposes is to be handy, to compliment him when he performs well, and to counsel with him when he is less than what he could be. You should know that we will be alert to teaching moments which will cover any or all the points of the Scout Oath, the Scout Law, the Scout motto, and so on. He may get cold or wet. He may not have the best food—he's going to be cooking some of it, you know. He may get a cut finger or get dirty. We will be having those experiences together on our camping trip. We will ask him at times to take care of us. We all will, at the same time, be alert to take care of him properly. Every one of those challenges will be developmental while we learn to be better people one with another, including your son."

Third Challenge: Giving Talks

An interesting challenge is how to get boys to give talks on Sunday without reading what someone else has said. The answer, or at least one answer, is to take them camping. A boy can use the experience to formulate a talk before a church audience. Giving a talk can be traumatic for boys who are not very articulate, and most boys are not. Let's suppose a talk is asked for, and the quorum adviser and Scout leader is involved. He says, "Bill, it's about your turn to give a talk. Could we invite you to do so next Sunday?" The boy will likely protest, "No way, I can't do it." The follow-up could be something like this: "Bill, I'll help you write up a report of what we did on our last camping trip. For example, who were our worst cooks? I think the audience would like to know about that. You could say something about how we appreciated Mom's cooking, couldn't you? Was there someone in the group who seemed to help out more than others?

Was there someone who was especially fun to be around? How about something funny that happened? What special things did we learn about? Was there a new kind of bird or flower that we identified? What about the songs we sang together around the campfire? Do you remember anything about the Scoutmaster's Minute at the close of the campfire? Could you mention that as you give your report? Could you mention our closing prayer together and how close we felt to our Heavenly Father?"

Most boys will respond under such circumstances and perform using such an approach. The next time the boy is approached to give a talk, it will be easier. Some boys fear to give public talks to such an extent that it is a reason for boys becoming inactive. A Scoutmaster needs to be aware of this and work especially carefully with such boys. The following words represent typical boys' feelings about giving talks: When a group of teachers quorum boys were asked if any of them would like to be called as a General Authority, one of the boys spoke up and replied, rather forcefully, "Who'd want to go around and give talks in church every Sunday?"

Fourth Challenge: Responding to Peer Pressure

The challenge of how to use peer pressure to promote behavior in favor of gospel purposes is a most significant one. We have observed that peer pressure can be the most dominant force boys face and to which boys respond. Many studies support this premise. To become a more effective force than that which comes from peer associations is an enormous challenge for any adult who has had occasion to rub shoulders one-on-one with a boy. If you build a better mousetrap, the world will beat a path to your door, Emerson once said. Peer groups are formed when boys lead other boys in doing things that are a come-on for them. They will likely be challenging, exciting, and stimulating activities. Often they are doing things that are on the edge in negative ways, actions that adults may say they ought not to do. In fact, one of the attractions of peer pressure involves experimentation with things that adults frown on. This can be countered by strong leadership and the offer of wholesome activities which invite boys to plan, talk, practice, and meet with one another to perform, explore, and do things together. If the quorum adviser and Scout leader knows how peer influences are created and managed, he will have great advantage.

Incidentally, many of you may have noticed the things boys talk about after they are released from the quorum meeting or Sunday School class. These topics are usually *not* extensions of the lesson and its importance. To intercept those conversations is to learn that they are usually about sports, such as a game that occurred the day before. It may be a special activity that they are looking forward to doing. They may be discussing the performances of a role model, which in most instances is someone who is skilled in some sport. One answer lies in creating activities in which those same boys are encouraged to perform as a group and to be with one another away from the classroom.

Fifth Challenge: Sharing the Gospel

How do we get boys to become missionary-minded? One answer is to have them invite their non-LDS friends to go camping with them. Reference has been made earlier to the fact that when the Lord spoke to the deacons, teachers, and priests in Doctrine and Covenants section 20 in 1838, he was speaking to men. In that reference, the words *teach, exhort, expound,* and *warn* were the description of efforts which were to be done by adults that held the aforementioned positions. With the young age of contemporary Aaronic Priesthood holders, this counsel is most difficult to follow. Scouting can become a catalyst for initiating an experience or exposure to gospel values and principles from a boy member to one who is not. As an example, your LDS boy and son can say to Bill, who is not a member, "Bill, we've got a cool Scout troop. We're going to have fun and do some great things. We're going on a camping trip in a couple of weeks. Our Scout leader is something else. You can't believe the things he knows and can do in the outdoors. Wouldn't you like to come along? Ask your folks if you can come." Your boy could accomplish a worthy goal by sharing the principles of the gospel in ways that are the modeling kind, the doing kind.

I believe it would be appropriate to mention that the sons of

Helaman may not have exactly been people who were talented in teaching, expounding, or exhorting. But they certainly must have been great at doing certain types of things. Of course, they also had great moms, and I'm guessing that they probably had great leaders besides Helaman—perhaps quorum advisers and men with skills not confined to the limits of a classroom, or to Sunday meetings for that matter.

Good quorum advisers and Scoutmasters can advance this process and pick up on opportunities to extend the circle of boy friendships to those that are the outer circle of the family. For example, non-LDS moms and dads can be exposed to the virtues of Scouting and to the roles that can be played by adults in the program regardless of religious preferences and indirectly become exposed to features of the gospel.

Sixth Challenge: Magnifying Callings

How can you get boy priesthood holders to magnify their callings as deacons, teachers, or priests? To magnify one's calling is easily associated with the words *power in the priesthood,* which is a common reference by many of us to that which occurs because of our priesthood commissions. Power connotes influence. For purposes of this representation, our answer would be to take priesthood holders camping. If those boys are practicing and learning how to live the Scout Oath, Law, and motto while camping, I promise you that they will be blessed. Certainly if they are not living the Scout Oath and the Scout Law, they will not be good deacons, teachers, or priests. More importantly, however, the boy will not be exercising the most precious of gifts of the Spirit, including that which is termed power in the priesthood. One would need only to be reminded of this by referring to Doctrine and Covenants 121:36–46. Exercising power in the priesthood can certainly be identified as a very positive influence that one boy may be exerting upon another. If power can be defined as exerting influence that causes others to live, obey, and follow the principles of the gospel, is this not a true exhibition of a boy magnifying his priesthood calling?

To illustrate, let me tell you a story. There were 130 of us camped on the South Fork of Yellowstone Lake. These were all Explorers, and we had towed canoes to the spot from the Thumb. It was to be an adventure of camping and canoeing. It also included bears, not unlike Bishop Eberhardt's experience referenced in an earlier chapter. After a sleepless night of hollering and banging of kettles, the morning came, and shortly after reveille was sounded, a boy was scratching on my tent. Troubled and with tears showing and in a faltering voice, he said, "Brother, I've lost my knapsack. It was right beside me by the tent when I went to bed." I announced the loss of the knapsack to the camp, and a tentative search was made in the near surroundings, but the knapsack was not found. As the day progressed, here was the boy back at my tent. His face was broad and smiling. The knapsack was in his hand, and he announced with special pride that he had found his knapsack. I was delighted, and I said, "Where did you find it?" He said, "I went away from camp after breakfast and prayed to Heavenly Father, and then I searched some more, and then I found it." Say what you will about the story. One cannot deny that the boy had been fortified by the power of prayer.

16

To Be Called and Chosen

There is a challenge in getting Scout leaders to be called but also chosen. One answer is found in making sure the leader understands what the purposes of going camping are for him. Again, I repeat that those purposes include providing situations, teaching moments, and intersocial relationships that will teach values. The outdoor camping adventure then becomes a laboratory for the priesthood, a teaching tool for boys to become self-reliant and skilled in saving lives, building an appreciation for and learning about the conservation of our natural resources. Teaching and providing boys with opportunities to lead and follow are included. Encompassing all of those is the anchor that Scouting provides in the development of effective values and Scout ideals as they are meshed with the purposes and principles of the gospel.

To illustrate this point, anyone listening to a symphony orchestra will recognize the skill and the enormous responsibility of the conductor in managing the harmonization, leading each instrument together in perfect time rhythm. When everyone works together to accomplish that common goal, a symphony of sound is created that becomes an exhibit of musical perfection.

A quorum adviser and Scout leader has a similar opportunity. In truth, he becomes a maestro, a director of a symphony. But rather than musical instruments, his instruments are boys. His encompassing challenge is to take boys into activities and seek from them all of the virtues, skills, and behavior patterns that are anchored to the excitement of Scouting and at the same time the performance of living gospel principles. One who is called and challenged to be a leader of boys can become a great maestro of the gospel.

In identifying those leaders who help priesthood quorums reach their objectives, the following four requisites are apparent. First, the quorum adviser and Scout leader is a doer, and he takes time to do things with his boys in addition to his work in the classroom. A second requirement that will help a quorum adviser and Scout leader is empathy. In other words, does he like being around young people? The third requisite is a testimony of the gospel. The kind of testimony that is needed by the adult leader is the kind that requests and receives from a leader complete dedication to his or her calling. What one says in testimony meeting on the first Sunday of each month is not the criterion for this test. No man knoweth truly, regardless of his public pronouncements, if he does not give evidence of being willing to lose himself in the service of his Heavenly Father. It is this kind of man who will perform within the fullness of his priesthood calling when it is added to baptism, Sunday meeting attendance, Church membership, and so on. Finally, fourth, is he likable? Can boys get along with him? If the boys say he's a nice guy and they like him, that's it. It is my belief any man in the Church can be a great leader of boys, if he possesses these aforementioned qualities.

Bishops Monitor Progress of Youth Leaders

We have described the importance of tenure. There should be a probational understanding between a leader and his bishop. If the leader, after having received training, is not doing his job or is not happy after having given his best effort for a few months, then he owes it to himself and the boys to go to the bishop and say, "I'm not performing as I know the Lord would like me to." The average tenure for those who were the leaders of the very best posts, to which we have referred, was six-and-a-half years. Many of our young men have lost years of precious achievement while the bishop waited hopefully for someone to fulfill his Scout calling. An enormous waste has taken place, multiplied many times over because that which boys missed may never be retrieved.

Reassigning positions of leadership would give both men a new chance. For the failing leader this may come because the Lord is willing to find another way for him to serve. The bishop's peace of mind comes in knowing that some of his boys did not slip away into inactivity because the new leader is willing to lose himself in the service of others, and he is assured that he is providing a quality program for boys. A bishop should be as nervous about calling a youth leader as a man that is caught in a thunderstorm with his arms full of lightning rods.

Stake Aaronic Priesthood Committees

The theme "Come, follow me" provides an appropriate application for those who are on stake Aaronic Priesthood committees. They help by seeing that boys get assistance in magnifying their performances in being deacons, teachers, and priests in each ward in the following ways. First, they help each Aaronic Priesthood quorum receive a planned opportunity to practice the application of gospel activities on a stake level away from home and away from the chapel. That occurs on other days besides Sunday and involves wholesome, challenging activities which boys like to do and which can be done with adult priesthood Scout leaders. Stake leaders can be great catalysts in encouraging the activity-type experiences that can be presented to boys by their ward leaders. In fact, there are many events that can be sponsored by the stake leadership and promoted by the local Scout council. The council, without exception, will welcome the leadership influence that can be generated by stake leaders in order to make those types of activities successful and productive. Stake leaders can help adult priesthood and Scout leaders in each ward see that the essence of Scouting is to help a boy's priesthood commitment by following the Scout Oath and Law, thus helping to ensure for the boy the guidance of the Comforter. Stake leaders should clearly understand this very important undergirding that Scouting gives to a boy's priesthood experience.

Second, stake leaders can help ward priesthood and Scout leaders to minimize just the telling about spiritual strengths that Scouting offers to a boy. Instead, modeling is encouraged as they lead youth into the practice of the ideals of Scouting while doing exciting things with boys. By stressing the importance of being trained to use the Scouting method, stake leaders can help ward leaders be more effective. Stake leaders could well remember that they themselves have spent years being trained in how the gospel should function before they were called to accept non-Scouting leadership positions in the stake. They should understand that it is important that the ward leadership for which they are responsible should attend training sessions conducted by the Scout council to learn how to conduct their Scouting responsibilities. In fact, such training could well become a personal responsibility for stake leaders. They should magnify their priesthood callings by learning how to use such an important tool as Scouting to help hold boys closer to the Church.

Finally, stake leaders can help each member of Scout quorum units in each ward understand that how they perform reflects well or poorly upon other non-LDS Scout groups as well as upon the district and area of the Scout association or Scout council to which they belong. For each ward unit to do well brings admiration from non-LDS boys and leaders as well as admiration for the Church and for all of its members. To do poorly with Scouting tarnishes efforts to interest others in the Church. In the relationship that the Church develops with Scouting, cooperation is required and obligations are established which ask for the best by the units of Scouting in the wards. Assistance also comes from local Scouting councils and associations as well as other sponsors; all are interested in the same ideals and goals of the Scouting program. There is a mutual responsibility for district and area Scouters to work in harmony with each other in providing the best for boys in every Scout unit, both LDS and non-LDS. The stake leaders can do much to help unit leaders in their wards recognize this important factor and to perform in ways in which they themselves model this kind of cooperation.

Importance of LDS Scout Leaders

Why is it paramount to provide LDS Scout leadership for LDS boys who are interested in Scouting? Some have promoted the idea that if a boy cannot for some reason receive the Scouting experience from his ward leaders, he could get that same experience from leadership provided by another sponsor. Sometimes LDS boys feel, for defendable reasons, that the Scouting in their ward is so uninviting that they would prefer to accept membership in another troop sponsored by another organization. Concurrently ward leadership could entertain the thought that if there is a Scout unit accessible, why become bothered with organizing a Scout unit in the ward? The answer is clear and unmistakable. This should not be a recourse for an LDS boy and should not be encouraged by ward leaders or parents. The LDS Church believes that the first part of the Scout Oath is, of all the ideals of Scouting, the most important for LDS boys: "On my honor, I will do . . . my duty to God" explains why all of our Church presidents have encouraged every boy to gain the Scouting experience. The Church believes that every Church leader who has a responsibility to work with boys of Scout age should become familiar with Scouting and secure as much Scout training as possible.

It is true that the Church appreciates and is grateful for the effort of any Scout leader who believes in God, regardless of his religious preference. But the Church also believes that a boy's Scout leader, if he is LDS, can better handle this very important purpose of Scouting. Non-LDS Scout troops and their leaders may and do interpret differently what a boy's duty to God can be. In the LDS faith, for example, there are some distinctive activities which the Church hopes a boy will consider as part of his duty to God. One of those is keeping the Sabbath holy. An LDS boy pledges to perform certain acts of service to other members on Sunday and to worship our Heavenly Father during a period of time on that day. The LDS boy is taught to place loyalty to father and mother first, then to the family and its goal to be eternal, as well as to the Church, and then to Scouting.

In many Scout associations, the leadership concept that Scouting should be the first consideration is not unusual. This is not to suggest that Scouting is to be neglected in the LDS concept, but it does place a clear priority as to where boys must direct their loyalty and their effort. There is no betrayal of the meaning of Scouting and its emphasis when those priorities are established and maintained. Such priorities provide clear and direct support for a strong Scouting effort by ward leaders. Within the confines of leadership responsibility, the priesthood should come first in any measure of responsibility, then Scouting. Thankfully, our General Authorities encourage combining the positions of quorum adviser and Scout leader, thus making it a jointly held responsibility. The blending of the strength of Scouting and the priority of priesthood is easily managed, understood, and accepted by the boy.

Another factor which supports the precious strength of having an LDS man as the Scout leader of LDS boys is tied to the Word of Wisdom. The charge to live free from habit-forming and harmful drugs and stimulants is part of the Word of Wisdom and serves as an important guideline for living. Those factors find placement easily and automatically within the recipe and behavior that Scouting provides.

A significant blessing and advantage provided by the LDS Scout priesthood leader is the encouragement he can and should give each boy to seek the educational and self-developmental aims of Scouting in such a way that they can and will be used to help the Scout become a better missionary. As a boy moves toward missionary age and as he absorbs the opportunities and development of leadership experiences, he will acquire skills and abilities that should significantly improve his missionary performance. Also, the leader has a modeling opportunity to help boys recognize the importance of choosing an eternal marriage companion.

Such leadership is not within the purview of a non-LDS leader and therefore would be absent. It becomes apparent that the non-LDS Scout leader finds it difficult to guide and counsel an LDS boy in those religious matters and to conduct activities for his group that will fit LDS needs.

In situations in which an LDS Scout unit has enlisted membership of boys who are non-LDS, the concepts just examined will need to be adjudicated by the leader. Great care will need to be taken not to take advantage of direct precept presentation, unless the non-LDS boy expresses interest with parental approval. This does not, however, negate the opportunity for modeling, which may rub off on him in ways that provide a respect for LDS beliefs and principles.

One of the greatest expectations for any bishop is to have all members of his Aaronic Priesthood quorum fulfill missions. Scouting, when it becomes part of the program of each Aaronic Priesthood quorum, provides opportunities for young men in many situations to feel close to their Heavenly Father and to feel the Spirit of the Comforter. Those feelings place him in a frame of spirit that encourages him to do his duty to God by fulfilling a full-time mission. Many times lessons and even activities are forgotten, but the spiritual feelings are remembered.

17

Scouting's No-Tomorrow
Syndrome

Webster defines *syndrome* as an aggregate of symptoms that indicate a special condition. A callous use of the definition allows me to introduce some popular phrases that liberalize Webster's definition. You are familiar with many of them. They are: "Do it now." "Get with it." "Good intentions are not enough." "It is the here and now that counts." "The proof of the pudding is in the eating." "A bird in hand is worth two in the bush." "Seeing is believing." "Put your money where your mouth is." And one that cannot be assigned to a modernism but which is as applicable today as it was two thousand years ago, "Faith without works is dead" (James 2:20).

There is a syndrome that is truly applicable to Scouting. I call it the no-tomorrow syndrome. This no-tomorrow syndrome asks a boy, "Did you do your good turn today?" Another example is "Learn to make your fire with two matches because at the next campout two is all you'll get." It is found in the counsel, "Make your pack lighter because by that fifth mile it will be very, very heavy." It is the merit-badge counselor who, after teaching all the techniques of the life-saving merit badge, tells the boy, "Now to pass this merit badge, you must swim out and bring me back to shore." Scouting can be very unforgiving, and purposefully so for a boy under certain circumstances. It can be a board of review when a member of the board may say, "We think you had better come back next month. Your patrol needed you for their service project, and you weren't there."

It may receive a broader interpretation when the Young Men president says, "Can we hold up Bob's Eagle rank? Last night Sister Jones attempted to control a disturbance he was making in Mutual, and he behaved very badly toward her." It is the Varsity team coach who says to his crew leader and star forward on the ward basketball team, "I understand you were giving Sister Forsyth a bad time in Sunday School. Just what does it mean to you to do your duty to God, to be faithful in your religious duties?"

It was also exemplified by a non-LDS Scoutmaster of a world-jamboree troop. He had been with the troop, most of whom were LDS, in an early-morning priesthood meeting at which Elder Marion D. Hanks of the Seventy was presenting some thoughts to us. The Scoutmaster asked me if I had noticed the behavior of two of our boys. I answered no, and he said that they were not paying attention, that in fact they were disturbing those around them so that even others were having difficulty trying to hear what Elder Hanks was saying. He said, "I think I would like to talk to them. Would you feel all right if I did?" "Certainly," I said. He replied, "You had better be with me, I believe." So he called them into his tent; I was there. He said, "You know I am not LDS, but I am ashamed of you. I'm disappointed in you. Your actions were certainly un-Scoutlike during Brother Hanks's talk. I feel I ought to apologize to Brother Hanks for you and for this troop. If you do not go to him and personally do so, I will certainly go and apologize for you."

Scouting can become a marvelous foil for any church where a boy's behavior needs immediate improvement, where things can't wait to become better. The Church's patience concerning a boy is very long-range; it is often long-suffering. If the Church does not impact a boy's behavior to change, it continues to be forgiving and invites the boy to come back tomorrow. However, when a boy needs help, it may be wise for the leader to take off his Church coat and put on the Scouting one, which enables him to say, "I'm sorry, time's up. You must shape up and give a better performance. You are embarrassing us."

I have shared with you application stories for this learning experience that I have termed the no-tomorrow syndrome in Scouting. They are true and real. One other example is a story about a Scoutmaster and a troop of boys from Richmond, California. The Scoutmaster's name was, appropriately, Sam Eagle, and he was a brilliant engineer. He was newly appointed for a troop of boys sponsored by the Richmond Lions Club. The boys had had some experience and a brief introduction to Scouting previously, but they were still untrained Scouts. At an early Sunday-morning hour, my home telephone rang. When I awakened enough to finally reach the phone, the time was about 4:00 A.M. and the voice on the other end announced, "Thane, Thane, I'm sorry to awaken you if I did, and I suppose I did. This is Sam Eagle." And I said, "Yes, you did, Sam." He said, "I think this is important enough that I should interrupt your rest. In fact, it is overwhelming for me, and that's why I've called."

This was his story. He had taken his Scout troop to a camp in Marin County managed by the Scout council headquartered in the city of San Francisco. The camp was a beautiful spot. He and the boys were excited about the prospects for a weekend of great fun. But upon his arrival he received an urgent message from his business office in Sunnyvale, a town down the peninsula from San Francisco. The message stated that his presence was required. He could not refrain from complying. He left the boys in the charge of the camp, explaining to the camp leadership what had happened. The camp counselor assured him that they would try to take care of the boys while he was away. Many hours later, when Sam arrived back at the camp, he was told that all of the boys of his troop were locked up in the Marin County jail.

Sam continued unfolding the events of the day. As it turned out, the camp was understaffed. They didn't have the personnel to be with the boys, and the boys wanted to go hiking. The boys were given a map and some instructions, were turned over to their patrol leaders, and were allowed to leave the camp with hopes that they would follow the directions diagrammed on the map given to them. As the hike progressed, the heat became oppressive. The dusty, tired boys all at once came upon a beautiful body of water. There were signs saying "No trespassing" along the shore of this small lake. But

the cool water was irresistible to them, and the boys decided to take
a quick dip. Having thus been served, but quite un-Scoutlike, they
were preparing to quickly leave the site of their transgression. However, at this very point the patrolman for the conservation district
happened upon the scene and found the boys swimming in a source
for the San Francisco water supply! It was no mystery to me as Sam
unfolded the story why, when he returned to camp, he found that his
boys were all locked up in the Marin County jail. Because of the
timing of the phone call and the evident concern that it had generated for me, my wife, Pal, had snuggled up to the earphone and had
caught the essentials of Sam's message. Typical of her, and I suppose
of wives in general, she whispered, "Oh, I hope they are not too severe on the boys. After all, cleanliness is next to Godliness."

When Sam finished unfolding the story, he simply said, "Mister,
I called you because I just wanted assurance from an answer to a
question. Is this one reason why I'm asked to be a Scoutmaster?" I
paused and thought about that inquiry. On the other end of the
phone, Sam waited patiently without any other explanation of the
question. Finally I said, I think to my credit, "Yes, Sam, I suppose it
is. In fact, I'm sure it is." He said, "Thank you, Thane," and hung up,
and that was all.

I was very anxious to learn the outcome of that situation. I tried
to reach Sam the next day and couldn't locate him. The second day I
succeeded, and immediately with great anxiety I said, "Sam, what
happened?" He said, "Things are all right. The boys are out of jail.
We're going to manage fine. In fact, I think things are taken care of
pretty well." He continued, "You'll be interested to know that there
are twenty-three boys in my Scout troop who are on sort of a probation schedule with the Marin County sheriff's office. Their probation
is related to special training sessions in the merit badge for public
health. I want to assure you that there are twenty-three Richmond
Scouts who will receive the most complete and thorough training in
the requirements of that merit badge of all the boys in all the troops
of the city of Richmond, California."

The no-tomorrow syndrome that is offered in situations that are
peculiar to Scouting is one that Scouting does not apologize for. In
fact, it is a very great plus when it is brought to bear properly upon

the experiences of boys who must grow into manhood in ways that are wholesome and complimentary to their parents, their church, and their leaders. In Sam's final report to me about the situation, he also mentioned, "You will be interested to know that the merit-badge counselor in this instance is the sheriff of Marin County. I think I can assure you, Thane, that all twenty-three of those boys are now very impressionable. I am looking for opportunities for teaching moments that will provide learning experiences for both this Scoutmaster and his boys, moments that will teach what it means to be a Scout." I have never lifted a glass of water to my lips on occasions when I have been thirsty in the area of San Francisco without having entertained a deterrent impulse which caused me to pause, momentarily at least, as I envision twenty-three dusty, dirty, sweaty boys having washed themselves clean in water which I might possibly be drinking. I am also tempted to expand occasionally on the brief interpretation of the point of the Scout Law that says a Scout has clean thoughts, clean habits, and travels with a clean crowd, by adding something about not cleansing himself in drinking water.

18

Good Samaritan

It is appropriate to mention some personal feelings which are generated whenever I have been privileged to associate with a group of LDS men who are performing as Scout leaders of boys. I have not shared this companionship when such men are gathered together without it generating a deep and abiding conviction that such a group is very special. If they are trained and have been active, I believe them to be as well acquainted with our Heavenly Father and his handiwork as any group could be. Their boys love them because they are wise to some of the things that only God has a patent on: the celestial pattern of a wild columbine, the marvelous symmetry and beauty of a blue spruce, the tireless yet musical chatter of a mountain stream, the beckoning of a tall ridge and the trail that leads to a place where all the winds meet. Surely such leaders are sensitive to the agony of the heaven as it foals a summer thunderstorm and to the related miracle from heaven as the storm breaks and reveals a sky unbelievably stamped with an arch of many colors, sometimes reflected in lakes nestled in perfect spots in the mountains of the Lord. Have they not seen his footprints where the scarlet paintbrush flames? Have they not heard, through the song of the meadowlark in the morning and the hermit thrush at twilight, his voice upon the air? Have those men, in the stir of the wind that shakes the aspen leaves beside the brook, not recognized his hand light upon their brows?

Have they not caught the glow of his robes where the last fire of the sunset burns?

To shake hands with men such as those is to shake hands with men who have, in very appropriate and practical ways, advertised to all that the satisfactions of life are not to be found only in one's interest in personal gain. There is a certainty that each one has, in ways that have been described and in others unmentioned, exhibited a flavor of greatness.

Vacation

He started off at dawn for summer camp—
How long he had been waiting for this day!
Our little lad, whose face still bears the stamp
Of babyhood; who has never been away
From home at night . . . who heave a heavy pack
To boyish shoulders, sudden-squared with pride;
Departed, laughing, not once looking back—
I'm glad he didn't know his mother cried.

Dear Father-God, take special care of him—
He's very trusting, and he is so young.
Return him sun-bronzed sturdy-sound of limb;
With songs of wind and water on his tongue;
With friends, adventures, camp-fire dreams to prize;
With memories of mountains in his eyes.
—Ethel Romig Fuller

Luke makes reference to the principle behind all that we do in Scouting. The record describes a teaching moment the Master Teacher used to burn into the minds of his disciples the important meaning of a concept he wanted them to grasp. The setting was the night of the Passover, the Last Supper. The story as found in Luke 22 says that he spoke in this manner. "He that is chief [is] he that doth serve" (v. 26). Then we are told that Jesus washed the feet of his disciples.

This is my question to any and to all: Are not the greatest among us those who serve most? If a roll call of the great men of earth since time began were conducted, would it not be easy to document that

principle of their performance? To be more timely and more typical
of a Scouting concept, could I ask why you love, admire, and respect
some of your associates perhaps more than you do others? Is it not
found in your observance of their performance in the service of others?

There is another way to explain this. When involved in Scouting
activities, I often carry a coin that bears an inscription. It is sort of a
coin of the realm for a certain kind of boy. The inscription is a boy's
interpretation of the second of God's greatest commandments,
"Thou shalt love thy neighbor as thyself" (D&C 59:6). In color it
matches that of the Golden Rule. There is printed on one side *On my
honor, I will do my best* and on the other *To do a good turn to someone each day.*

Elder Vaughn J. Featherstone relates the following experience:
"Years ago I had the opportunity of traveling to Pocatello with Elder
Marion G. Romney of the Council of the Twelve. I was on the General Priesthood Missionary Committee of the Church. Between sessions of conference, Elder Romney and I walked several times
around the parking lot. It was a cool, blustery, overcast day. As we
walked, all of a sudden President Romney stopped, turned to face
me, and said, 'Brother Featherstone, do you think the brethren of the
priesthood will ever come to understand that they were born to serve
their fellowmen?' Everything in my soul responded to that principle.
I knew it was true. The purpose of the priesthood, Aaronic and
Melchizedek, has been, and is, and always will be to serve God's
children here on earth." (*The Aaronic Priesthood and You* [Salt Lake
City: Deseret Book Company, 1987], p. 8.)

When I am in attendance with a group of men who are there because of dedication to the Scouting effort, I never cease to sit in awe
and wonder of that which they represent. The warm glow of the
meaning of the parable of the Good Samaritan reaches out across the
centuries from Galilee. I am certain that I can hear that greatest of all
teachers interpreting the efforts of such men: "Inasmuch as ye have
done it unto one of the least of these my brethren, ye have done it
unto me" (Matthew 25:40). "And when he putteth forth his own
sheep, he goeth before them, and the sheep follow him: for they
know his voice" (John 10:4). "And he saith unto them, Follow me"
(Matthew 4:19).

19

Boys and Christ

Up to this point, we have examined those men who, in accepting leadership positions, have said to boys, "Come, follow me." We have not examined the direct interpersonal focus of a boy of priesthood age as he may internalize his relationship to the Savior. It can and should be a very personal one. Nor have we examined in much detail how the father of a boy of priesthood age may literally say to him, "Come, follow me."

In the instance of a boy's earthly father, we have noted the enormous challenge and the significant failure of some earthly fathers to provide effective modeling for boy followership. Because of the intimate relationship between boy and father, it is in the fifth step of the learning process—application—when the father can be really effective. The other steps—exposure, repetition, understanding, and conviction—usually involve dialogue, and all are of limited help when worthy performance by the father is not visible. It is the performance, the modeling, by that earthly dad that can provide a clear-cut pattern which the son may follow.

In the invitation that a boy receives from the Savior to follow him, we recognize that we can as teachers and leaders act as helpers and catalysts to bring about that relationship. We must sustain the hope that we have challenged the boy to order his life in a way that the Comforter may find a dwelling place with him and in so doing promote the oneness between Savior and boy which will be the most precious of all experiences a young man may acquire.

I have submitted only a limited examination of how those whose stewardship may involve the wholesome growth of boys may promote a boy–Savior relationship. Certainly one of the major problems in helping young people reach out toward the Savior and seek his companionship is related to how well we as teachers and leaders teach a boy about and of him, how we teach a boy to perceive him. We must show how the Savior can and will fit into the patterns of a boy's daily activities and his common interests, not just his Sunday ones but as a companion available to boys regardless of the day or the activity. We can help by teaching boys to accept the Savior as a constant, positive person in their lives. We can teach them to see him as someone who approves of and is pleased and interested in all wholesome, youthful activity. As quorum advisers and Scout leaders, we can promote a spiritual atmosphere in which our young people can accept the Savior and love him as they love their earthly parents. Leaders can provide opportunities for boys to generate a personal oneness with the Savior by encouraging a personal, visual image of him, one which may include features that are expressive and meaningful. Most boys will welcome the imagery that suggests perfection of body, of muscle, of stature. That leads to other capabilities that can add comfort and will encourage oneness with him. Athletics is a first for many boys in that regard. If a boy perceives that his performance as an athlete, whatever field it may be, is one that is looked upon with encouragement by the Savior, the boy's athletic performance is enhanced. Young people should know that he approves and is observant of a boy's mathematical ability, musical interest, or scholarly achievement. We can carefully build an understanding that whatever and whenever he's doing something that is worthy, the Savior is proud of him.

On one occasion, one of our respected recreation professors whose specialty was dance at BYU overheard me asking a class of college students if they pictured the Savior as a skilled ballroom dancer. I noticed his extreme interest, and after the class I asked if he had a similar conception. His response was forceful and immediate as he said, "Absolutely." Then rather facetiously, but I think with some sincerity, he continued, "I will be very disappointed if my mansion in heaven does not provide for good dancing."

If a young priesthood boy has a clear mental picture of what God is like and believes he is favorably sensitive to a boy's consuming interests, isn't it possible that the boy will find it easier to seek companionship with him? Isn't it likely that he will reach out to the Savior on the athletic field if he believes that the Savior is interested in all kinds of wholesome sports? If the Scout believes that the Lord has an athletic interest and is pleased when one plays with courage, skill, and fairness, will the Scout not seek a closer relationship with him on and off the athletic field? If a boy believes that the Savior is deeply concerned about the conservation and wise use of heavenly creations, isn't it likely that the boy will feel more responsible for the care and preservation of our mountains, rivers, and forests? Will not each young man as he becomes more conscious of the wonders and beauty of nature become interested in learning more about the Savior and his creations?

President N. Eldon Tanner on one occasion described a lesson he learned about getting boys acquainted with the Savior. Notice the broad application of the principle, regardless of the situation in which anyone may be involved: "Two or three years ago while traveling with Lord Rowallen, Chief Scout of the British Commonwealth, I was thrilled with his comment as he led a group of scouters in the Scout Promise. As he repeated 'On my honor I promise to do my duty to God' he paused and said, 'As I make this promise I think of a God who can and does hear and answer prayers, who is interested in what we are doing and who will guide us and bless us according to our needs and our faith.' And then he made this significant statement, 'If any of you cannot believe in such a God, you can serve better some place else.'" (Conference Report, April 1963, p. 102.)

In other words, Brother Tanner was using his conversation with Lord Rowallen to say, if you don't have a belief in God you can't be a good Scout leader. In our priesthood and Scout work, the Savior says to a boy, "Come, follow me" in all of his performance opportunities within the program of the boy's priesthood and Scouting experiences.

I am grateful to one of our great prophets of this modern era, President David O. McKay, who opened up our vision to accept the fact that a desire for an immediate special spiritual experience may not come as hoped for as boys or adults. The following story reinforces the need for all of us to help our boys have faith that the Lord is sensitive to their needs but chooses when their needs will be met. It also requires a recognition that no single facet of our efforts is likely to produce for our Aaronic Priesthood young men a special advantage in the Melchizedek Priesthood, with its great promises and covenants.

I listened as a boy to a testimony regarding the principles of the gospel, the power of the priesthood, the divinity of this work. I heard the admonition that we, too, might get that testimony if we would pray, but somehow I got an idea in youth that we could not get a testimony unless we had some manifestation. I read of the First Vision of the Prophet Joseph Smith, and I knew that he knew what he had received was of God; I heard of elders who had heard voices; I heard my father's testimony of a voice that had come to him declaring the divinity of the mission of the Prophet, and somehow I received the impression that that was the source of all testimony.

I realized in youth that the most precious thing that a man could obtain in this life was a testimony of the divinity of this work. I hungered for it; I felt that if I could get that, all else would indeed seem insignificant. I did not neglect my prayers, but I never felt that my prayer at night would bring that testimony; that was more a prayer for protection, as I look back upon it now, to keep intruders away—really it was more of a selfish prayer—But I always felt that the secret prayer, whether in the room or out in the grove or on the hills, would be the place where that much desired testimony would come.

Accordingly, I have knelt more than once by the serviceberry bush, as my saddle horse stood by the side. I remember riding over the hills one afternoon, thinking of these things, and concluded that there in the silence of the hills was the best place to get that testimony. I stopped my horse, threw the reins over his head, and withdrew just a few steps and knelt by the side of a tree.

The air was clear and pure, the sunshine delightful; the verdure of the wild trees and grass and the flowers scented the air; as I recall the incident, all the surroundings come to me anew. I knelt down and with all the fervor of my heart poured out my soul to God and asked him for a testimony of this gospel. I had in mind that there would be some manifestation, that I should receive some transformation that would leave me without doubt.

I arose, mounted my horse, and as he started over the trail I remember rather introspectively searching myself, and involuntarily shaking my head, said to myself, "No, sir, there is no change; I am just the same boy I was before I knelt down." The anticipated manifestation had not come.

Nor was that the only occasion. However, it did come, but not in the way I had anticipated. Even the manifestation of God's power and the presence of his angels came, but when it did come, it was simply a confirmation; it was not the testimony. . . .

But the testimony that this work is divine had come, not through manifestation, great and glorious as it was, but through obedience to God's will, in harmony with Christ's promise, "If any man will do his will, he shall know of the doctrine, whether it be of God, or whether I speak of myself" (John 7:17). (David O. McKay, "A Personal Testimony," *The Improvement Era*, September 1962, pp. 628–29.)

Paraphrasing President McKay, it is my testimony that we find that Scouting "embraces principles of life everlasting." When used as a laboratory for the Aaronic Priesthood, it will help to "distill upon the soul a benediction of the Holy Spirit." As with President McKay, I know that it will help sons be "good citizens" and add to "their obedience to the promptings of the gospel (*Ibid.*)."

If I could summarize all that has been presented in previous chapters, perhaps I could use the reminder of Elder Matthew Cowley when he spoke of the meaning of the word *integrity* and how its application was significant in the performance of boys who hold the Aaronic Priesthood. He suggested that to build integrity for the priesthood is a long process, not an instantaneous one. That it is. It often requires patience and the acceptance of performances a bit at a time, without becoming discouraged. It may involve a leader working faithfully in his calling, recognizing that Saints aren't usually made overnight and that boys may not be made into Saints, even over the years. This suggests that the long-range expectation on the part of our Heavenly Father is that in our responsibility we must not give up. We must sustain a constant effort to encourage within the boy the desire to follow him, even though at times the trail may be hard to find and the first steps may be hesitant. If he has become lost, we must become handy to help him find it again and encourage him though the way may seem too steep and ask for too much.

> I never loved your valleys
> Your shaded country lanes
> your pleached alleys
>
> I want my hills
> the trail that scorns the hollow
> Up, up the ragged shale where few do follow
>
> Up over wooded crest and jagged boulder
> with strong thigh and heaving chest
> and swinging shoulder.
>
> So let me hold my way
> By nothing daunted
> Until at break of day
> I stand exalted
>
> High on my hills of dream
> Dear hills that know me
> And then how fair will seem
> the lands below me.
>
> How clear at even tide
> the church bells chiming
> God give me hills to climb
> and strength for climbing.

One of the greatest expectations for any bishop is to have all members of his Aaronic Priesthood quorums fulfill missions. Scouting, when it becomes part of the program of each Aaronic Priesthood quorum, provides opportunities for young men in many situations to feel close to their Heavenly Father and to feel the Spirit of the Comforter. Those feelings place him in a frame of spirit that encourages him to do his duty to God by fulfilling a full-time mission. Many times lessons and even activities are forgotten, but the spiritual feelings that were felt are longer lasting.

There is a story about a grove of redwood trees botanically identified as *sequoia dendron giganteum* found on the western slope of the Sierra Nevada range. It is a story that helps one understand how Scouting may embellish the work of the Aaronic Priesthood quorums in the LDS Church. That grove of redwoods is located not far from a little town known as Angels Camp, made famous in days past by the exploits of Joaquin Marietta, a rather infamous Mexican bandit, and the jumping-frog stories of Mark Twain. Those trees lie in a protected ravine today known as the Callivaras Big Trees State Park. In the early 1850s a party of lumbermen-turned-goldseekers came upon this grove of redwoods as they were scouring the sands of the North Fork of the Stanislas River for gold. The grove contained the largest living things of God's creation. Those giant trees towered more than two hundred feet above those who discovered them. The base of one tree approached forty feet in diameter and was once used as a dance-hall floor. Perhaps because fortune had eluded them, they saw in the largest of those trees a chance for fame, albeit an unworthy one.

Nonetheless, they were determined to cut the huge tree down to be able to say that they had cut down the largest tree that ever grew. Using techniques developed in cutting down the giant kauri trees of New Zealand, they labored for twenty days, using augers and a system of wedges until their work was almost completed. Then they decided, "Why not find some others to see this famous event?" So they left the scene with the tree still standing and traveled down the canyon to Angels Camp to spread the news of the possible spectacle of witnessing the greatest tree in all the world fall to earth. A great crowd followed them back, but as they came near the grove a resounding roar came rumbling down the canyon. Some said a rush of wind accompanied the sound as the earth trembled beneath their feet. Curses and other words of frustration were hurled about by some in the party, for they were certain they knew the cause of the disturbance. Sure enough, when they broke upon the scene of their labors of the past three weeks, there lay that giant redwood, that monarch of the forest, which had, as Edward Markham described a felling of a tree, "gone down with a great shout upon the hills and left a lonesome place against the sky" ("Lincoln, the Man of the People," in *One Hundred and One Famous Poems,* ed. R. J. Cook [Chicago: Cable, 1926], p. 156). None were there to see it fall except those little forest animals whose ancestors had lived within its shelter since the Savior walked the earth.

Some say that it was divine justice that intervened and robbed the perpetrators of the pleasure of witnessing that which they would destroy for the sake of destruction. For it is a true axiom that no one should tear down except to use for a better purpose the fruits of their destruction.

I am not acquainted with all of the forces that were operative in producing that grove of giant trees. I know only that they are there, that I have stood beneath them; I have looked up and up and up and up and have declared that they just could not be. Yet there they were, unbelievable evidence of God's handiwork. I have thought of them as being among the noblest of God's creations. There is evidence that he exercised much patience in their growth and that he used a combination of special conditions which encouraged their development. Certainly they were destined in the very beginning to have special qualities.

The Lord has introduced Scouting to the LDS Church because it is designed to use special forces and because it can create special conditions that will cause a den of cubs, a troop of boys, a team of Varsity Scouts, or a crew of Explorers to become uncommon like a grove of redwoods. Scouting can help produce among boys monarchs of our young men. If we do not bring special forces to bear that in a parallel produce redwoods of boys, there are other forces less worthy that will bring a boy down upon the hills and leave a lonesome place against the sky, a place where he might have stood as the noblest of God's creations.

It is my testimony that Boy Scouting is an inspired program. There is no better place for it than to have it help the Aaronic Priesthood of the LDS Church hold boys close to the Church and help cultivate their spiritual growth that they may remain faithful in doing their duty to their Father in Heaven, in serving others, and in keeping themselves among those that are the noblest work of God.

Conclusion

If you and I have spent some time together with this book, you know that since 1913 our prophets, seers, and revelators—that is, our Church presidencies and Apostles—have asked us to use Scouting to help enrich and bring vitality to the purposes of the Aaronic Priesthood. The Doctrine and Covenants designates unequivocally the special responsibility of the bishop of each ward to manage and direct the Aaronic Priesthood. Although Scouting per se has not been canonized officially within the standard works as part of the Aaronic Priesthood, subsequent authoritative literature and verbal pronouncements have given it semiofficial status. It is a latecomer as a segment of the restored gospel, and in being so it often becomes vulnerable when ward and stake administrators have failed to recognize the contributions it can offer to the program of the Aaronic Priesthood. Its requisites, if it is to function properly, are anchored in the selection of quorum adviser and a Primary Scout leader who must be stalwarts among Saints and regard their calling as though the Savior were saying to them, "Pick up this cross, and follow me." They must be shepherds for a boy when he turns eleven and must continue to lead and guide him through his deacon and teacher and priest ages. Thus fortified, the boy becomes a more worthy candidate for the Melchizedek Priesthood, qualified to exercise the power and authority offered to him by that sacred commission.

If you are a Primary Scout leader or a quorum adviser and Scout leader, you are aware that you have become part and parcel of the designation given to the bishop wherein you serve in his presidency of the Aaronic Priesthood and that thereby you also are responsible for the wholesome development of every boy within the ward. You have become aware that the essence of Scouting is the spiritual development which it can add to the Aaronic Priesthood experiences of every boy. You particularly must become a laboratory instructor who may help unfold into the application and activity of each quorum every principle of the gospel a boy will have an opportunity to practice. You will certainly be a model of behavior that reaches into every waking moment of his life—his Sundays, his weekdays, his associations with his friends and his peers. In fact, in you he may see some pattern for his life and all that it projects for him, including a mission, marriage in the temple, and faithful service to others throughout all his mortal tenure.

I trust that in the reading you will accept the offer of Scouting to help internalize its ideals and thus reward parents, peer associates, and our Father's purposes for restoring the gospel in these latter days through The Church of Jesus Christ of Latter-day Saints.

So I commend this book to you. Examine it as something that may add a little luster to the jewels in the crown of the restored gospel and recognize that when Scouting is given direction and purposeful use, it becomes a rewarding catalyst to our efforts to achieve the purposes and objectives of the Aaronic Priesthood and the LDS Church. In the words of President David O. McKay, "God bless us all with these ideals of Scouting, which are the ideals of the gospel of Jesus Christ" ("The Good Turn," *The Improvement Era,* February 1963, p. 77).

Index

About the Author

Dr. Thane J. Packer pioneered the early development of university curriculum designed to prepare young college graduates for executive leadership with the Boy Scouts of America. He holds degrees from Brigham Young University, the University of Utah, and Utah State University. He has served as the assistant Scout executive in Berkeley, California, and as the Scout executive of the Cache Valley Council in Logan, Utah.

Dr. Packer taught at BYU until 1981, when he was awarded professor emeritus status at the university. In 1982 he accepted an assignment from the LDS Church and the Scouting association to help develop a Scouting program in New Zealand. This assignment was later expanded to develop programs in Tahiti, Fiji, Tonga, and Samoa.

Dr. Packer has written extensively about Scouting for the LDS Church. He served for eleven years as a member of the General Boards of the Church for the MIA and the General Aaronic Priesthood Committee and was a member of the team that developed the Varsity Scout program.

He is the recipient of the Silver Beaver and Silver Antelope.

Dr. Packer and his wife, Palmyra, are the parents of two sons and two daughters and have thirty grandchildren.